Read What Others Have To Say. . . .

"No vague service theory here! A clear, no-nonsense approach on how to effectively deal with difficult customers. A potent refresher course necessary for everyone in the customer service field."

Roy Devine, Customer Service Dept.
Data Media Products, Inc.
Chicago, IL

"The risk of losing a valuable customer is only one emotional phone call away. This book is a sobering reminder of how we all must examine and refine our behavior management skills when dealing with the public who pay our salaries."

James Scova, Group Sales Manager
Venture Communications, Inc.
New York, NY

"A powerful learning package for both public and private service providers. Not only easy to read and operate, but an invaluable sourcebook for learning the critical interpersonal communication skills necessary for good public relations."

Robert Wendover, President
Leadership Resources, Inc.
Denver, CO

"From road rage to workplace violence, service providers suffer from an epidemic of emotionally dangerous people. A superb approach for teaching anger diffusion and conflict management. An essential book for continuing education programs on both the corporate and college campus."

Stephen Powers, Ph.D.
Psychology Department
University of Arizona

UPSET CITIZENS & CUSTOMERS

HOW TO DEAL WITH THE ANGRY, DIFFICULT, DEMANDING PUBLIC

*A Customer Service
Guidebook for Government
and Business Service Providers*

UPSET CITIZENS & CUSTOMERS

HOW TO DEAL WITH THE ANGRY, DIFFICULT, DEMANDING PUBLIC

*A Customer Service
Guidebook for Government
and Business Service Providers*

THE EVERGREEN PRESS
EVERGREEN, COLORADO

The Evergreen Press
P. O. Box 4181
Evergreen, Colorado, 80437
Telephone: (303) 670-3335   Fax: (303) 670-8418

Printed in the United States of America

Limit of Liability/Disclaimer of Warranty

Sales Inquiries/Quantity Discounts

Substantial discounts are available to government agencies, corporations, professional associations, and other organizations. For information, sales, distribution, or bulk quantity discounts, contact the publisher at the above address.

Upset Citizens and Customers: How to Deal with the Angry,
Difficult, and Demanding Public
by
Donald W. Slowik

LCCN: 98-93582

Publisher's Cataloging-in-Publication

Slowik, Donald W.
    Upset citizens and customers : how to deal with the angry, difficult and demanding public / by Donald W. Slowik. – 2nd ed.
    p. cm.
    Includes index
    ISBN: 1-883342-08-2

    1. Customer relations. 2. Business communication. I. Title

HF5415.5.S56 1998   658.8'12
                           QBI98-1285

FIRST EDITION, 1998

Table of Contents

Introduction

CHAPTER ONE
The Basics of Customer Service

CHAPTER TWO
The Value of Self-Esteem

CHAPTER THREE
The Power of Listening

CHAPTER FOUR
Behavior: The Foundation
of Successful Service

CHAPTER FIVE
Maintaining Customer Service
During Negotiation

CHAPTER SIX
The Difficult Situation:
Handling Anger

CHAPTER SEVEN
Managing Stress and Burnout

CHAPTER EIGHT
Damage Control

CHAPTER NINE
Customer Service
On the Telephone

CHAPTER TEN
Customer Service on the Internet

Introduction

"No one makes you inferior without your permission."
— Eleanor Roosevelt

Who is This Book For?
Why is This Book Valuable For the Employee
    and the Employer?
How Does This Book Differ Substantially From Others?

Whether you provide services directly to the public on a regular basis or whether you only represent your organization sometimes, you need to possess the communication skills that enable you to manage the interaction while you simultaneously work to achieve your objectives. Serving the public is not a natural talent in today's individualistic society. On the one hand, we are taught that our feelings and reactions are valid, but when managing interactions with customers, we find ourselves having to suppress our natural emotional responses to negative events.

What this means is that behavioral control is essential to the success of any service provider. Whether your job is to make a sale, provide informational services, or help people who have complaints, you will be more likely to achieve your goal if you project the professional image that garners the respect of others. This book, *Upset Citizens & Customers*, describes behavior techniques that can help you project that desired image. Minute changes in the way you interact with others can completely change the way in which you are perceived. Even something as simple as how you break eye contact can have potentially devastating effects on how your customers perceive you.

As a service provider or representative of your organization, the behavioral information provided in this book can be invaluable. Not only will it help you to interact more effectively with the public, but these skills can also be used for your professional and personal advancement. It can also make the workplace a safer place for you and your co-workers.

Today's service providers are faced with a daunting task. They must give friendly and efficient service, while simultaneously trying to defuse confrontations, soothe ruffled feelings, and act as mediators and master communicators, all while maintaining professional demeanors in keeping with their organizations' images.

That's a lot to ask of anybody. But it is not an impossible task, particularly when certain logical, easy-to-master techniques are used.

There are three basic things that every person involved in an organization should remember:

1.   The fact that no one is actually complaining

doesn't mean things are perfect. You may simply be failing to get adequate feedback. Research shows that people who complain are actually more likely to come back than those who are unhappy and who do not complain.

2.   Everybody needs to watch their behaviors. Even those who don't interact with customers a lot need to learn to manage their behaviors effectively. This leads to better working conditions for everyone in the organization.

3.   Satisfaction, not just service, is the responsibility and goal of a service provider.

Who is This Book For?

This book is for virtually anybody who has to deal with the public. It is designed to help service providers such as:

- Administrative planners
- Bank employees
- Call center personnel
- Computer service providers
- Customer service representatives
- Educators
- Elderly care providers
- Emergency services personnel
- Food service providers
- Government employees
- Hospital personnel
- Hospitality personnel
- Hotel service personnel
- Law enforcement personnel
- Medical professionals

- Public relations personnel
- Retail salespeople
- Sales professionals
- Security personnel
- Service managers
- Telephone operators
- Transportation industry employees
- Utility workers
- You

While its primary focus is on improving interactions between employees and the public, it is also valuable for those who face confrontational or stressful work situations with co-workers.

Why is This Book Valuable For the Employee and the Employer?

It doesn't matter what business you are in – if you deal with the public, you need to provide good customer service. Whether you are a restaurant employee, a city worker, or a teacher, you will benefit from the strategies in this book. Your employer will benefit from an improved image, a loyal customer base or satisfied clientele, and improved cost-efficiency. But the employee also reaps rewards, because there is less conflict and stress in the workplace. In addition, employees with good customer service skills are generally more likely to get positive recognition from their supervisors, resulting in more promotion opportunities and higher pay.

How Does This Book Differ Substantially From Others?

While some books acknowledge that good relations with the public and customer service are communication issues, they rarely focus on the specific information you need to become a better communicator. This book does. But, rather than bore you with a lot of theory, this book focuses on the information you need – actual strategies, the "do's and don'ts" you need to know to be most effective in customer service.

Communication is more than just the words you choose. Your body reveals numerous messages to others, and sometimes this can damage your credibility with members of the public, with your co-workers, and with your supervisors. The lessons you'll learn about nonverbal behavior will help you in all facets of communication – not just in customer service.

Furthermore, this book focuses on the customer and public service arena as a whole. Rather than working to improve one aspect at a time, you can improve behaviors and skills that apply to the activity in its entirety. Customer service is not something that can be practiced by just focusing on the customer. Everything that takes place within your organization can impact your success as a service provider. If you are in a position to help your company plan or develop in-house training, the information provided here can be invaluable to your decision-making process.

EDITOR'S NOTE: Dr. Donald Slowik was a founder and president of Chicago-based London House Inc., a nationally prominent human resource training and psychological testing firm. With over 25 years of experience, he has authored more than a dozen books and publications and developed numerous training programs in the fields of personnel interviewing, interpersonal communications, and human resource development. An active instructional designer, Dr. Slowik researches in the fields of multi-disciplinary interviewing, conflict resolution, and interpersonal communication techniques. He has an MA in corporate security management and a Ph.D. in administration and management.

CHAPTER ONE

The Basics of Customer Service

"He that plants thorns must never expect to gather roses."

– Pilpay

What is Customer Service?
Why is This About Health, Well-Being, and Survival?
Why Good Service Starts With Attitude
How Does a Positive Attitude Translate Into Good Service?
What are the Basics of Customer Service?
What Do People Want From You?
Do Grace and Charm Come With Age and Experience?
What are the Major Things to Think of When Serving the Public?
What You Can Do to Improve Service

What is Customer Service?

You don't need to have a lot of experience to provide good customer service, nor do you need to have a thick skin and a rule book that spells out what you should do in specific situations. All you really need to do is communicate professionally and never, ever take things personally.

Providing good service is important to whatever organization you work for, whether public or private. There is good reason for this – good relations with the public provide your organization with increased sales and fewer costs; a happier, more loyal clientele; and a good image. But, while these are all very important considerations, employers often forget to mention the most important reason of all – your personal physical and mental well-being.

Why is This About Health, Well-Being, and Survival?

If you learn to communicate positively and professionally with members of the public, with co-workers, and with supervisors, you will decrease the level of stress you encounter and make your working environment a more safe and pleasant one. It decreases confrontational situations and will probably make you more satisfied with your job. At the same time, it meets your employer's objectives and satisfies the customer's needs and concerns.

The issue of safety in the workplace cannot be understated, however. You don't need to look far to find examples of how communication can misfire, sometimes with tragic results. We have all heard tales and read news accounts of people who were pushed just one step too far. Many times, the ultimate victim and target of these people turns out to be a person who is simply doing his job and trying to balance customer service with the needs of his company or agency. Most of these violent situations could have been averted by simple communication techniques that will be described in this book.

Another reason good service benefits you involves your future. Even if you don't intend to stay in your current position, performing your job well has countless rewards, the most prominent being good relationships with people who will provide references and be character witnesses to your prospective future employers. When you provide good customer service, you are telling others that you care about people, you care about your job, and you care about your future. If your future is at your current organization, you are likely to ensure better pay and quicker promotions. By doing your job well, it reflects well on your supervisors and, more often than not, this will make your work environment more pleasant, and your future with your organization more secure.

Why Good Service Starts With Attitude

The statement "you've got to have a good attitude" is made so often by our parents, teachers, and employers that it has almost become a cliché. But take a look at your co-workers, friends, and acquaintances. Which are generally the happiest and most satisfied – the ones with good attitudes? Or the ones who are always negative?

People with good attitudes generally get further in life for one very simple reason – people are more likely to help them or, at the least, not stand in their way. People with negative or indifferent attitudes are erecting barriers in front of themselves. Their attitudes won't stop them completely from meeting their goals, but they are inadvertently and unnecessarily making the journey more difficult.

How Does a Positive Attitude Translate Into Good Service?

When it comes to serving the public, attitude has a direct consequence. Those with a good attitude towards their jobs and their roles are more likely to successfully manage complaints and problems. This is because your attitude is reflected in everything you do, and it is apparent to the person you are interacting with. Even if you say all the right things, the other person might leave with a negative impression, because your nonverbal behavior can transmit your real feelings or distaste for the interaction. You can smile and answer questions truthfully, but you may lean away from the person or fail to make eye contact, encouraging the customer to believe that you are insincere.

When you have a good attitude, you are more likely to display supportive nonverbal behaviors, and this can go a long way towards reaching your service objectives. The plain truth is that not everybody is immediately suited to customer service. Some jobs, for instance, demand that you be assertive and authoritative. When changing jobs, it would be extremely difficult to automatically switch to such service-oriented behaviors as friendliness and accommodation. But when you understand that it is your behaviors that are causing your discomfort, you can begin to change or modify your behaviors according to your needs. More information about how your verbal and nonverbal behaviors can help or hinder you will be presented in Chapter Four.

The attitudes of employees play an enormous role in an organization's overall success. Those people who approach the process positively create something that can't be bought at an office supply store or through a catalog – customer loyalty. Optimistic, energized, and loyal employees are invaluable, and these are behaviors that must come from within – they cannot be taught. These attitudes can be

Memo to the Boss

Good attitudes among employees start with you. How an employee treats a customer is similar to the way you, the boss, treat the employee. If you work hard and communicate well with your employees and the company's customers, your employees will emulate you. To promote customer loyalty, you must be loyal to your employees. Don't act like you hate your job – it will only make your employees hate their jobs. Don't lose your temper – you only show your employees that it is okay for them to lose their tempers. You set the rules. If you follow them, so will the majority of your employees.

self-developed, however, by people whose skills give them confidence.

What are the Basics
of Customer Service?

There are three phases when service of one form or another takes place:

> **Phase One. Advance Preparation** – Often, the need for service can be anticipated and handled in advance. This type of pre-servicing can include the preparation of documentation or it can involve pre-training of personnel so they understand their role and the products they sell or services they are to perform. The purpose of this type of preparation is to solve problems before they occur and make sure the public is getting what it truly needs and wants.

> **Phase Two. The Initial Contact or Sale** – The needs of the public must be met. If people get what they need, desire, or expect in the first place, the chances are greater that they will be satisfied.

> **Phase Three. Afterwards: When Problems Arise** – Usually, when a customer or member of the public contacts your organization after the sale or after the service is provided, it means that something has gone wrong. This is when your service skills will be put to the test. Organizations which provide good service at this stage can ensure satisfied, loyal customers.

Regardless of which phase of customer service you are involved in, there are three rules every effective service provider follows:

> **Rule One. Know Your Stuff** – Before you can pro-

vide good service, you must know what your objectives are. A social worker's objective might be to help people find short-term housing. She would need to know about the local housing situation, costs, and availability. She would need to know who she could serve and where to send people for help when she can't serve them. A post-sale telephone service provider might need to know how to help a customer repair or adjust a product or help the customer locate a service shop. Each provider will have different rules, policies, and procedures. The bottom line, however, is that you must be prepared before you can provide effective service.

Rule Two. Look at the Situation From the Other Side – In order to provide the best service possible, you must understand how things appear from the other side. How would you feel if you didn't have a home? What would you think if you spent thousands of dollars on a computer only to find out it doesn't work? It's easy to go "by the book," but, sometimes, the best service requires you to improvise.

Rule Three. Respond With the Appropriate Behavior – In many service situations, your behavior is far more important than whether you give the customer what he wants. If you make an honest, sincere attempt to help your client – and he knows it – the client will probably be satisfied and go away with a positive impression of you and your organization.

These rules should be applied during all phases of the interaction. Once these rules are clear, the Seven Steps of Positive Service are easier to manage. These steps are:

1.   **Mental Preparation** – Approach the interaction positively.

2. **Listen** – Be patient. Look for hidden and unspoken meanings.

3. **Respond** – Ask questions and give feed-back.

4. **Understand** – Use the given information to assess the whole problem, which may be more than the customer first revealed.

5. **Assist** – Fix the problem if possible. Do what you can do for the customer.

6. **Verify** – Make sure the customer under-stands the instructions for fixing a problem and make sure that all his concerns are met as fully as possible.

7. **Conclude** – Finish the interaction without rushing.

Later in this book, after you know more about positive and negative behaviors, we'll look at how you should behave during this seven-step strategy.

What Do People Want From You?

When people look for service from the government and private organizations and companies, their expectations are incredibly – and tragically – low. Surveys show that people don't expect service providers to be either effective or efficient. For the service provider, this is both good and bad. It is good because any time you provide good service, you will pleasantly surprise your customers and clients. But it is bad because this attitude makes the public reluctant to call for service and, when they do contact you, they are usually aggravated before they even walk in the door or pick up the telephone to make the call.

So, what do members of the public want when they contact your organization for service? Help. It's as simple as that.

There are several basic components the public looks for in getting this help, and an organization's success or failure in addressing these components impacts how positively or negatively the public perceives an organization. These components include:

1.   Wait Time
2.   Ease of Access to Service
3.   Quality of Support
4.   The Behavior of the Service Provider(s)
5.   The Results of the Contact.

Wait Time – Wait time is a vital component in that, if it is excessive, it only aggravates the frustration of the customer or client. A good example of this is retail sales during the busy Christmas holidays. Sales personnel can attest to the fact that Christmas cheer decreases exponentially the closer people get to the cash register. This is caused by the difficulty people have in getting things done in all the crowds. First, they have to battle for parking spots, then they have to jostle through crowded stores and compete for the time of sales personnel. Finally, as a reward, they often have to wait in long lines before they can spend their hard-earned money.

The same frustration applies to any situation in which a person has to waste valuable time waiting for service. A customer who is put on hold is just as frustrated as anyone who waits in line to get help. Wait time does not apply only to the number of times the phone rings before it is answered. It also includes the amount of time it takes for the customer to actually get the opportunity to speak to a real person. Elaborate phone systems which require people to navigate several menus before getting to a human service provider can sometimes add to the client's level of frustration, depending on how the system works.

Easy Access to Service – If customers find it easier to get help with their problems, they tend to be more satisfied. Documentation, clearly posted phone numbers, and Internet pages

Knowing When to Improvise

A bank has a policy requiring that customers cannot receive account information over the phone. One customer has a problem, because he needs to know how much he was paid in interest during the previous year, and he has lost the form sent to him by the bank. After leaving several messages for the proper person at the bank, he gets no response. Finally, in frustration, he calls the complaint department, explaining that he needs the information right away or his taxes will be filed late. The customer service agent listens to him describe the frustrations he has experienced in trying to reach someone in the records department. She knows the problem is caused by a combination of a new, untrained person on the job and demands of the busy tax season. But she understands the customer's frustration and, after verifying the identity of the customer according to bank policy, she makes an exception to the company policy and gives the information over the phone.

can help clients get necessary aid. Additionally, toll-free numbers provide easier access than do long-distance numbers and can help ease costs and frustrations for customers.

Quality of Support – Employees who know their jobs well and interact confidently with the public can help improve customer satisfaction. Internet pages for those who like to help themselves can be effective, but so can personal support for those uncomfortable with technology. Image can mean a lot in this area, because a professional approach will be better received than a grudging response – even if the results are the same. Furthermore, service providers should be aware that clients expect more from "big names," and they should be careful to meet the public's expectations for their products or services.

Behavior of the Service Providers – Customers need to feel that they have your full attention and interest. Your body language, vocal tones, and word usage should be carefully orchestrated to communicate that you care about helping them. One of the most vital aspects of managing your behaviors involves your listening skills. This subject will be addressed more fully in Chapter Three.

Reaching a Conclusion – Naturally, customers will be more satisfied when they contact you and you are able to help them reach a resolution to their problem. It is important that the problem be handled as thoroughly as possible during your interaction – whether in person or over the phone. If it is not possible to do so, the client must be clear on the status of the action to be undertaken, and he should know how to reach you – the same person – again, if necessary. You are that person's advocate – his contact with your organization.

Remember that the customer doesn't really care why something went wrong – he only really cares about results. It may be the only time your product ever failed to work properly, but the customer doesn't care about the product's record in relation to other customers. He only knows that he spent a lot of money and received a defective product.

Do Grace and Charm Come With Age and Experience?

Grace and charm are often byproducts of age and experience, however, you don't have to wait to acquire these characteristics. All you need to do is learn to manage your verbal and nonverbal behaviors so that people perceive you to be more credible and likable.

Whether you are handling a complaint, making a sale, or helping a member of the public comfortably access government services, you must build some sort of a relationship with the customer. This can be difficult, particularly between people of two widely divergent backgrounds. The following skills are helpful for any interactive situation.

- **Be at Ease** – A person who is relaxed and

comfortable is easier to approach and can interact more easily with others. On the other hand, a person who is stiff, tense, and has an aloof attitude will find the communication process to be much more difficult to manage.

• **Talk About the Things that are Personally Important** – If a communicator does not express his or her needs, others cannot help fulfill those desires. This does not mean that you should monopolize the conversation.

• **Be Discreet** – Discretion is as important as honesty. The possession of knowledge is not an excuse to impart it. Carefully consider the ramifications of the information before you reveal it.

• **Listen to Others** – Effective communication cannot take place if it is one-sided.

• **Ask Questions** – This gets the conversation going (or keeps it going).

• **Be Curious** – Find out what makes the other person tick. People generally like to talk about themselves, and this will give valuable insights that may be useful to you in current and future interactions.

• **Be Sincere** – People can tell when they are being manipulated, and they don't like it.

• **Don't Force Personal Views on Others** – Avoid being overly forceful in getting a personal viewpoint across. Even those who share similar beliefs and opinions can be turned off by statements that are expressed too strongly.

- **Use Impression Management Skills** – The way you handle yourself during a conversation will impact how you are perceived. Clothing, vocabulary, and nonverbal cues will influence your success.

What are the Major Things to Think of When Serving the Public?

How would you want to be treated? That is probably the most important thing you need to keep in mind, no matter who you are trying to talk to. This involves following some basic rules about getting along with others:

- Perceiving others accurately
- Being truthful
- Practicing tolerance
- Being sensitive to inner meanings
- Listening empathetically

Perceiving Others Accurately – Because we interpret the world differently from those around us, it is important to develop the ability to see others as they really are and not how our initial – and not necessarily correct – perceptions tell us to see them. It is necessary to see past labels and stereotypes and base our interactions on reality.

Being Truthful – Honesty facilitates open and effective communication. Failure to be truthful slams barriers into place that can be incredibly difficult to overcome. Avoid exaggeration and never lie to a customer.

Practicing Tolerance – Tolerance is a respect for the differences of other people, their beliefs, and practices. Tolerance can be developed by a person who actively seeks differences and then makes an effort to overcome the problems caused by them. It is often help-ful to look for similarities among the differences. This common ground can help facilitate the communication, because the chances of misunderstanding may be reduced. To be tolerant, one must learn to accept without making judgments and without trying to impose one's own views on another. Honesty, openness, and respect are key com-ponents of tolerance, as is avoiding a "superior" attitude. The tolerant person is open to change.

Being Sensitive to Inner Meanings – At times, what a per-son actually says and what his intended message is are two entirely different things. This tendency can be a particularly acute problem in the customer service arena, because you cannot satisfy a person unless you understand what the real, underlying problem is – if there is another level of meaning.

Listening Empathetically – An empathetic person is one who can let others know he is truly interested in them and that he wants to hear what they have to say. He does not interrupt, rush to conclusions, or judge and will probably check back with the speaker to make sure he received the message correctly. The empathetic lis-tener attempts to truly understand the viewpoint of the other person in the communication process.

What You Can Do to Improve Service

The following are some general guidelines designed to help you manage service interactions with typical members of the public:

Things To Do

- Act in a professional manner at all times – don't take things personally.

- Listen, listen, and listen.

Are You Taking Things Personally?

If you hear yourself saying things like this, you might be taking things personally and not professionally:

- "I don't get paid enough for this."
- "Why me?"
- "They don't appreciate me."
- "I don't make the rules."
- "It's not my fault."
- "Don't blame me."
- "I didn't do it."

- Consider the situation from the customer's point of view – be empathetic.

- Understand your service goal – know what your role is, and understand what the customer's or public's expectations were and how they are not being met.

- Be positive – focus on the good.

- Always be honest.

- Choose the right words – don't inadvertently aggravate the public.

- Try to keep the conversation on track.

- Respond immediately to a problem.

- If the customer is aggravated, try to calm

things down before beginning to work on the actual solution.

- Always let the customer know what you are doing, particularly if you must leave for a moment or are silent for a time.

- Identify yourself immediately. If a customer asks for your name again, state your name and spell it without further prompting.

- Write down pertinent facts so you don't have to ask the customer to repeat information.

- Speak slowly to help calm the customer down and to help manage your own stress level.

- Compliment the customer in an appropriate and sincere manner.

- Try to ask close-ended questions that require only a "yes," "no," or one- or two-word response.

- Follow up – make sure the customer feels that he received good service.

- If you are not sure how to help the customer, tell him so and seek assistance from someone who can help.

- Be willing to make exceptions to rules if the circumstances seem to warrant it.

- Stay courteous.

- Focus on the problem.

- Be aware of how you are communicating nonverbally.

Things To Avoid

- Don't take things personally – always act in a professional manner.

- Don't erect communication barriers.

- Don't interject your opinions.

- Don't rush – make sure the public feels like you want to take the time to help.

- Don't make the customer wait.

- Don't interrupt – allow the customer to say his piece.

- Don't be afraid to seek help from your supervisor with difficult interactions.

- Don't let the customer's behavior keep you from addressing his problem.

- Don't use vulgar language – your good behavior in the face of another's unacceptable behavior will encourage the other to improve his actions.

- DO NOT be judgmental if the other person uses vulgar language or behavior. Allow your good behavior to provide a low-key example.

Chapter One Summary

This chapter was meant to provide you with a general picture of the customer service process. But it is only a foundation upon which to build. To become a truly effective service provider, you must do two things: Become a good, empathetic listener (as described in Chapter Three) and develop an awareness of how your verbal and nonverbal behaviors can impact your success (as described in Chapter Four).

Key elements to remember from Chapter One include:

√   Be as knowledgeable as possible about your job, its variables, and the people you serve. Know how far you can go in order to meet your service objectives efficiently, effectively, and fairly.

√   Understand how the process appears from the public's point of view.

√   Respond with the appropriate behaviors in a professional manner.

√   Never, ever take things personally.

√   Remember that you are doing this for your own health, safety, well-being, and future.

CHAPTER TWO

The Value of Self-Esteem

"Confidence is a plant of slow growth in an aged bosom."

William Pitt, Earl of Chatham

A Driving Force in
the Human Character

One of the most valuable things you possess is your self-esteem. Self-esteem is a driving force in the human character. It influences the way we perceive ourselves and the way others perceive us. It can also greatly impact the successes in our lives. People who maintain a high sense of self-esteem are able to accomplish more simply because of their inherent vitality and strong self-confidence. They achieve their goals more quickly and more fully, and they tend to be happier and more satisfied with their lot as a result.

People who lack a healthy self-esteem often put roadblocks in front of themselves without realizing it. They actually prevent themselves from achieving the things they desire most. When people think they "can't" do something, that they don't "deserve" something, or that they aren't as "good" as others, they are setting themselves up for failure.

Self-esteem gives you the confidence and self-assurance you need to persuade others to help you meet your objectives. But this self-confidence is a fragile thing. People are easily wounded, and damage done to a person's self-esteem is very difficult, if not impossible, to repair.

How Does Self-Esteem
Apply to Customer Service?

People with a healthy sense of self-esteem are better service providers than are those with a low sense of self-value. Thinking positively about yourself enables you to interact better with people. It is easier to focus on the real problem and not let personal issues hinder communication.

Positive self-esteem is also valuable because it promotes positive attitudes, which are vital to providing good customer service. As a service provider, you have to project positive images of yourself and your organization. To do this, you first have to have a positive image of yourself.

Everyone Has a Confidence Problem – Some of the Time

Doubting yourself is a normal part of life. Everyone does at times – the president of the United States, the Prince of Wales, the most famous of movie stars and athletes – self-doubt is simply a fact of life. It is a survival mechanism intended to make us recognize limitations and think before we take actions that could do us serious harm.

But self-doubt can be crippling if taken to extreme degrees. People who lack self-esteem often correspondingly lack the following:

- They lack the ability to bounce back from minor setbacks.

- They lack the ability to keep things in perspective. They may overreact to even minor thoughtless or unintentional words and actions of others.

- They lack the ability to contemplate the activities they must undertake in order to reach their goals.

- They lack the ability to learn from their failures and apply this knowledge and experience to help them ensure their future successes.

- They often fail to even attempt to reach their goals if the slightest possibility of failure exists.

- They often lack the ability to succeed even if they do make an effort, because they are already convinced they will fail. They set themselves up.

Do You Have a Low Sense of Self-Esteem?

If you have a low sense of self-esteem, it's almost certainly not your own fault. You are probably continuing an attitude that has been with you for your entire life. While there are many factors which contribute to low self-esteem, your personal childhood likely holds the root cause.

Children need to be praised and recognized for the good things they do by their parents, their relatives, their teachers, their friends, and anyone else with whom they interact. Even loving parents with the best intentions can damage a child's self-esteem in moments of irritation or through simple thoughtlessness. There are no "perfect" parents in this regard. However, these acts are only devastating to a child's ego if they happen frequently or are continuously reinforced. A child with a strong support system is better able to cope when confronted with the occasional non-supportive person he may encounter.

This attitude carries over into adulthood. When authority figures or others who are important to you berate you or make you feel inadequate in some way, you lose some of your self-esteem. But, again, if you have a strong support system, you can overcome this loss.

Additionally, we magnify our own failures internally. When we disappoint the people we care about the most, for example, we are often more disappointed in ourselves than the other person is. The other may quickly forget an incident while you continue to brood over it. People with positive self-esteem are eventually able to let go of these incidents, while those with low self-esteem often hang on to the failures and make them a permanent part of how they judge themselves.

Everybody fails at some things. Your support system from family and friends will largely determine how you ultimately respond to these failures. However, now that you are an adult who has taken responsibility for yourself, it is your behaviors that will influence the way others react to your failures. You can react positively or negatively – your friends, family, co-workers, and employers will inevitably take their cues from you.

Building Your Self-Esteem
by Respecting Yourself

You are worthy of respect. Every person on this planet is worthy of the respect of others. One of the major reasons people lack self-esteem is that, for some reason, they don't like themselves. Perhaps they've done things they are not proud of or they just don't seem to fit in.

Well, guess what? We've all said things we are not proud of. We've all said things we wish we hadn't. And we all feel like we don't belong at certain times and in certain situations. But this does not mean that we deserve less respect than anyone else. Self-doubt is a human emotion that everyone shares. It is a consequence of our intelligence.

As an intelligent person, you have the right to exist on your own terms. You have the right to form your own opinions and make your own decisions. The only person you really need to justify these things to is yourself. Understanding that you truly are the decision-maker in your life is the first step to improving your self-esteem. The opinions of others will always have an effect on you – there's no question about that – but, ultimately, you are the one who will make the critical decisions that will determine how you live your life. It's easy to make excuses for continuing to hold on to the attitudes, beliefs, and circumstances that are harming you, but, in the end, you are the responsible party.

Continue to remind yourself that you are a good person and worthy of respect. Remember daily that you are good at what you do. This type of positive reinforcement is invaluable.

Another Step – Time
for Self-Evaluation

Once you can truly understand that you control your own destiny, you can build up your self-esteem. If there are things you don't like about yourself, and if these things are damaging your self-esteem, you can change them. To do this effectively, you must undergo a brutally honest self-evaluation process (keeping in mind that you will always be harder on yourself than other people will be).

You are actually many people. You are a child, a parent, a sibling, a spouse, an employee, an employer, a friend, a relative, a partner, a sports fan. . . . The list is endless. Sometimes, you have to

Ask yourself the following questions about your family, your job, your interests, and your relationships with other people who are important to you. Consider how every aspect of these things impacts your self-esteem and the type of person you want to be.

- What will happen if I don't make any changes at all?

- Do I let things happen *to* me, or do I make them happen *for* me?

- Do I engage in activities I know are harmful to myself or the people I love or care for?

- Do I always take the easy route? Or am I willing to take appropriate risks to improve the things I encounter in my life?

- Do I let my relationships affect how I feel about myself?

- Do I let my relationships have negative impacts on the things I want out of life?

be several of these people at once. Each of these roles is merely one aspect of who you are. You will find that you have more control over how you behave in some of these roles than in others, but you can impact how others treat you by the way you behave.

- Am I being used by people? Or do I have friends and family who genuinely support and care for me?

- Do I use the people I care about unfairly?

- Am I sensitive to the needs of others?

- Are others sensitive to my needs?

- Do I let my relationships with others just happen? Or do I work at making them successful?

- Am I getting the most out of my relationships with other people?

- Do I use my free time for myself? Or is someone always making demands on me?

- Do I neglect some responsibilities in favor of other responsibilities or to give myself more free time?

Examine each aspect of your life. Try to decide whether you find it satisfactory or not. What would you change? What would you leave the way it is? You have control of your life, and you can make these changes if you really want to.

How Will Making These Changes Build Your Self-Confidence?

Once you have identified things about yourself that you would like to change, you can start taking the necessary steps to bring about these changes. For instance, you might decide that one reason for your low self-esteem is that you do not have enough responsibility in your job.

To be eligible for a promotion or change to the career you really want, you might need more education. Taking college courses would then be a step toward raising your self-esteem. Chances are that you will begin to feel better about yourself as soon as you enroll in them.

As you take these steps, you will invariably have some failures. But you will also have successes. Learn from your failures, but focus on your successes. It is your successes that will build your self-esteem and gain you the confidence you need to interact better with others.

How to Get Yourself Addicted to Self-Esteem

As a service provider, you have the task of projecting a positive image of your organization or agency whenever you meet with any member of the public. You cannot do this effectively if you don't first have a positive image of yourself. There are certain things you can begin doing immediately to help you build or fortify a positive self-esteem:

- Set reasonable objectives for yourself, and work towards achieving them.

- Be willing to take reasonable risks. Think them through, but remember that you can't move forward if you don't take any steps.

- Accept challenges as things that make life interesting. Imagine how boring life would be without them.

- Continue to grow – learn new things and have fun.

- Learn from your mistakes. If you don't like the way you feel after you do something, don't do it again, but don't beat yourself up over it either.

- If something goes wrong, treat it as a chance to learn rather than as a failure. Let it be the basis for positive experience rather than an excuse for negativity.

- Give yourself the time of day – Take the time for yourself to think, plan, and reflect on your experiences and how they can help you in the future.

- Plan. If there are things you want, don't just strike out blindly and hope you get them. Figure out what you will need to get where you want to go. You'll get there much more quickly and with a lot fewer problems if you have a methodical plan.

- Try to see things from the point of view of others.

- Talk to people. Don't wait for them to talk to you.

- Give yourself time to think before you speak, particularly when the stakes are high. You'll appear to be more intelligent, and you won't have to worry later about what you "should have" said.

- Be nice – do things for others now and then, and don't worry about whether or not they'll return the favor.

- Compliment others, but be sincere about it.

- Associate with people who have positive attitudes.

- Avoid stressful situations whenever possible and reasonable.

Behavior Characteristics that
Make You Look Confident

Confidence:

- Direct eye contact
- Chin thrust forward
- Gestures such as steepled hands
- Relaxed
- Leaning back with hands behind head or across back of another chair.

- Don't allow yourself to be negative. Instead, focus on the positive. It is difficult to curb negative thinking once it begins.

- When you catch yourself thinking a negative thought, immediately begin to look for the opposite, positive thoughts. Mentally use the word "stop" when you find your mind in this negative mode.

- When you get up in the morning, think of positive things and don't allow negative thoughts to influence your day.

- Don't dwell on the things you don't have. Concentrate on the good things you do possess.

Behavior Characteristics That
Make You Look as if You
Lack Confidence

Lack of Confidence:

- Downcast eyes
- Head hung down
- Indirect body orientation
- Closed body posture

- Dress in a way that is consistent with others with whom you interact in a given circumstance. This will lessen the likelihood that you will feel like a "fish out of water."

- Stay physically healthy. Exercise and stay in shape so that you can feel good about yourself.

You're Working on Your Self-Esteem, But Nothing Seems to be Happening

You spent your entire life thinking about yourself in certain ways. Now, you are trying to change. This isn't an easy thing to do. People are naturally resistant to change. It is always easier to stay with the known than to risk the unknown. You cannot change overnight, no matter how deep your motivations are. Deciding to change is the easy part of the process. Actually making the desired changes requires a lot of hard work and dedication. It will come only with time and patience.

Consider the addict's dilemma. No matter how much he wants to stop taking the drugs that are ruining his life, he can very rarely just stop using them. The physical consequences to this may even be fatal. He may have to cut back gradually over time. He may have to suffer from withdrawal symptoms. And he may have to spend time in a doctor's or hospital's care. He may suffer many setbacks along the way even if he truly has the desire and motivation to quit. A lot of drug addicts find it easier to give up and go back to the drugs and the demeaning way of life rather than to continue the painful process of quitting. But, for those who feel the end result is worth the means, the battle is worth it.

Rather than looking at changing your habits all at once, look at them piece by piece. Change one behavior at a time. Don't worry about the overall strategy – that will come in time as you build upon your example. The following paragraphs will give an example of how this works.

In this book, self-esteem has been strongly equated with self-confidence. Building self-confidence requires building self-esteem. Each feeds off the other. But you can build your self-confidence a step at a time in other ways, too. For example, if you behave in a manner that people take for self-confidence, then they will perceive you as being self-confident, even if you are really full of doubts. If you are continually perceived as being self-confident, you will gradually begin to see yourself in the same way.

Therefore, a step-by-step process for achieving self-confidence is to adopt the nonverbal and verbal behaviors that radiate to other people that you already possess confidence. By integrating just small behavioral changes as simple as the way you sit or hold your head or look people in the eye, you can ultimately reach your objective of being a more confident person in any situation. You will succeed, and your self-esteem will grow.

Whenever you have a setback, remind yourself that you are not "failing," you are merely acquiring valuable experience. Although it does take time, the conscious employment of behavioral modifications will eventually become a normal part of your nonverbal vocabulary. Your self-esteem will grow, because you know it is growing, and you are doing something about it.

Chapter Two Summary

Regaining or enhancing your sense of self-esteem is not something you can do overnight. It is a lengthy, difficult process, but it is well worth the effort. Yes, it will help you become a better service provider – but the personal benefits far outweigh the professional advantages you will gain. People with a positive, healthy sense of self-esteem have the ability to reach their dreams and goals. They have one of the most important elements required for obtaining any reasonable objective – and a few that may seem to be unreasonable or over-ambitious.

Too much self-esteem can be as damaging as not enough – arrogance and a lack of respect for other people are dangers you must work to avoid. But combining positive self-esteem with empathy and compassion for other people can help you become an exceptional communicator. Listening skills, the topic addressed in the next chapter, are also vital for this achievement.

Key elements to remember from Chapter Two include:

√   If you lack self-esteem, you probably set yourself up for failure without even realizing it.

√   You are the only person who can really control your life and the direction it takes. Take charge to change it <u>now</u>.

√   Low self-esteem begins beyond your control in your childhood, but it's up to you to change it now that you are an adult if you find that you don't have as much self-value as you need to be successful. You don't have to accept personal failure.

√   Try to establish a strong support system of friends and family that can help you build the self-esteem you need to succeed in the modern world.

√   You, like everybody else, are worthy of respect from yourself and from the other people in your personal and professional life. If you don't feel that you are getting due respect from others, it may be time to make some critical changes in how you conduct your life.

√   Self-esteem is built one success at a time. When you decide to start making changes, begin slowly. Eventually, your minor victories will add up and your self-confidence will flourish.

√   Never, ever take things personally.

√   Remember that you are doing this for your
        own health, safety, well-being, and future.

CHAPTER THREE
The Power of Listening

"The hearing ear is always found close to the speaking tongue."

– Ralph Waldo Emerson

The One Skill You Will Use the Most

The one skill that has the most impact on a person's success in dealing with the public is listening. One reason for this is readily apparent – you can't fix the problem until you know what it is. But, in public service, the focus on fixing the problem often creates a situation in which the customer can form damaging opinions of the service provided and the organization providing it. This happens because the service representative is not truly listening to the customer.

Frequently, the one problem a customer points out is only symptomatic of a larger problem that is being experienced. A failure to listen can be costly, because the customer may shortly return with another problem or, worse yet, he may never return. Instead, he might just decide to take his business elsewhere while spreading the news about the lack of attention he received. In the private sector, this can equate to lack of sales and customer revenue while, in the public sector, it can ultimately translate into funding decreases and department cutbacks of employees or services.

Listening vs. Fixing: The Role of the Service Provider

This chapter will focus first on identifying the things we let get in the way of good listening, and then on what we can do to overcome these barriers. By becoming a better listener, the average person will find that he receives a variety of rewards, because this skill can help with personal as well as professional relationships. It can help us avoid problems with our spouses and children while simultaneously increasing our work abilities and standings within our organizations. In the task of serving the public, good listening skills will make you more likable, which will make it easier for you to establish a rapport with the customer, handle his complaints, and help him meet his real needs.

Frequently, people just need to vent their frustrations, and they don't actually need anything from you other than a friendly, compassionate ear. If you try to "fix" the problem with this sort of customer, you will only aggravate the situation. Always allow the customer as much time as he needs to tell you what is making him unhappy, then try to move the interaction along to a successful conclusion.

So You Already Know How to Listen . . . Or Do You?

Most people think they are good listeners when, in fact, they are not. Listening is something most of us have never been educated in. What little we do know we picked up in self-defense over the years.

But listening is more than just the physical act of hearing – it is a communication process that requires practice and attention in order to be done effectively on a consistent basis. Furthermore, listening involves more than just hearing what others have to say. It also involves the act of observing and attending to the ways others behave as they speak. Failure to attend to the other person means that you may miss part of a message – or even all of it – if you fail to see a qualifying behavior. A person can modify his tone of voice, for example, to express pleasure in something, while simultaneously making a face that shows sarcasm or humor or irritation or tolerance or many other emotions that can change the original message. More information on nonverbal behaviors and how they relate to customer service will be presented in the next chapter.

What Do You Need to Know About Listening?

According to communication researchers, we spend 70 percent of our waking moments doing four different communication activities. That time is split according to the chart on the following page.

When we were children in school, we spent hours, days, weeks, and years learning to read, write, and speak well, and almost

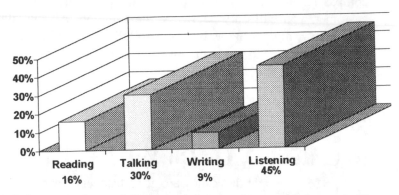

Reading 16%   Talking 30%   Writing 9%   Listening 45%

no formal time was devoted to the activity that we spend almost half of our communication time doing. Under those conditions, we probably shouldn't find it too surprising that we ignore, misinterpret, or forget 75 percent of the things others tell us. We are even worse at looking for a deeper understanding of what others are saying – the real meaning behind the words that are spoken.

Another Good Argument
For Getting Our Ears Cleaned

It is estimated that 80 percent of what we learn comes from listening – which means that, since we actually retain very little of what we hear, we are probably missing some pretty vital information. Listening is the act of hearing, understanding, and remembering, and we have three reasons for undertaking the task:

1.   **For Pleasure** – We feel this when we listen to beautiful music, the sound of a child's laughter, or the peacefulness of a forest.

2.   **For Decision-Making** – We need information to make judgments or evaluations.

3.   **For Specific Information** – Also known as discriminatory listening, we do this to get certain information that is important to us.

For example, we might listen to a long, rambling story even though we are only really interested in a certain segment. We listen to long, redundant graduation speeches only because we want to hear the name of a person we love.

All of these types of listening serve a purpose, and our goals are achieved more effectively if we are good listeners: We obtain greater pleasure, we make better decisions, and we are more likely to hear and recognize the desired bit of information out of all the other things we are being told.

Overcoming the 'Why I Can't Learn to Listen' Syndrome

To begin the process of becoming better listeners, the myths about the skill must first be examined and promptly discarded:

Myth One – Listening is a skill that can be turned on and off. People often believe that the activity of listening is something they can turn on when they really want to. In reality, this is rarely the case. The skills for listening must be learned and continuously practiced. The problem with this belief is that it is far easier to turn off your ears than turn them back on. Also, by the time you realize you are missing something important, it is often too late.

Myth Two – Intelligence Impacts Listening Skills. According to researchers, there is no true correlation between listening and intelligence. People who are intelligent are not better listeners, and people who are good listeners are not more intelligent. The reverse also is true. People who are less intelligent are not necessarily poor listeners, and poor listeners are not generally less intelligent. But one thing is true – poor listeners often are believed or perceived to be less intelligent. If you don't listen well enough to understand the question, then you are unlikely to be able to answer it in a thoughtful, intelligent way. And those who do listen appear to be more intelligent – they have more information with which to make decisions so, naturally, they tend to make the right choices more frequently than do poor listeners.

Myth Three – After you reach a certain age, you cannot learn to become a good listener. This is not true. Although learning is easiest for young people, this does not preclude adults from learning as well – as long as the adult wants to learn, that is. Becoming a good listener is merely an exercise in will-power and concentration along with the recognition and acknowledgment of your own personal bad listening habits.

These attitudes stand between people and their ability to become better listeners.

What Do People Do to Stop Themselves From Listening?

Everybody has different weaknesses and strengths when it comes to listening. Some people allow themselves to be easily distracted, while others are able to tune out the inconsequential events happening around them. The following is a listing of common attitudes that create barriers to good listening. Do you see yourself or someone you know when you read them?

Barriers to Effective Listening

Emotional Involvement – To many, politics (of whatever variety) is an emotional subject. They become so involved in "their side" of a controversy that they are unable to bear the idea of listening to the "other side." This harms communication because we may ignore a solution to a problem for the simple reason that it was put forth by the "other side," and we didn't bother to find out if it was a good solution. This is true whether the subject is office politics, family politics, or national politics. Allowing ourselves to get emotionally involved not only prevents us from listening but, in effect, gives power to others who have the ability to let reason replace emotion.

Exterior Distractions – It is not always easy to listen to others, even if we want to – a construction worker's jackhammer in the street may make listening to other people an exhausting prospect. Or, you may be so cold that you don't listen because you're too busy thinking about getting inside where it is warm. In situations like these, however, we usually are distracted because we are allowing ourselves to be distracted.

Inattention – If we are not really interested in the person or subject to begin with, or if we have a lot of other things on our minds, we may simply not pay attention to others. We may hear only parts of what is said and may be confused later about what information was actually received. Or, on the other hand, having heard something that did interest us greatly, we might be thinking so fast about possible implications that we fail to comprehend the continuing speech of others.

Indifference – If a subject bores us or is simply about something that is "not our cup of tea," it is difficult to make our minds receptive to the communication. Yet, sometimes, we must overcome this tendency. Practice, asking questions, and looking for reasons to be interested can help.

"My Turn" – The person who listens with a "my turn" attitude is not hearing what is actually being said. He is merely waiting for an opportunity to jump in and tell his side of the story. It is his anecdote or comment that he is thinking of, not the speaker's words.

No Common Ground – What would you say if you were meeting Great Britain's monarch? Nice hat? It must be interesting making a lot of state visits? What's it like living in a castle? If you have no common ground with another person, it's hard to have a meaningful conversation, let alone listen to the responses of the other party. Neither speaker nor listener is likely to be really interested in what is said.

Preconceived Notions – A common failure people have when listening is they believe that they already know what another is going to say. Or, we may "know" what the person is like, and we therefore expect to hear certain things. Basically, when we "listen" in these situations, our ears are open, but our minds are closed. Therefore, we are unlikely to retain any information that may be valuable to us.

The Speaker's Behavior – At times, the person with whom you are attempting to communicate is actually placing roadblocks in the way of understanding. Perhaps he mumbles or speaks with an unintelligible accent. Or, maybe it's his very delivery (an attacking, angry mannerism, for example) that turns us off. If we are truly interested in listening, we must learn to turn off our prejudices and avoid the easy solution of "tuning out."

Confusing Facts and Inferences – A fact is verifi-

Characteristics of Effective and Ineffective Listening

Effective Listening

Interested	Patient
Caring	Attending
Nonemotional	Responsive
Nondistracted	Sensitive
Other-centered	Understanding
Empathic	Alert
Noninterrupting	

Ineffective Listening

Disinterested	Impatient
Uncaring	Inattentive
Emotional	Nonresponsive
Distracted	Insensitive
Self-centered	Quick to judge
Apathetic	Bored
Interrupting	

able, whereas an inference is a probability based on other information. Even if the inference is based on a fact, it is not necessarily true. A communicator must maintain the ability to discern fact from inference even in an emotionally charged situation.

Speech/Thought Rate Disparity – People speak at 125-175 words per minute, but they think almost four times faster. Because of this, the receiver can sometimes think ahead and lose the train of thought of the sender. If his mind wanders, he could miss valuable information.

Other Poor Listening Habits – Most people train themselves in listening, and as a result have developed habits they usually perform automatically and without conscious thought, such as faking attention.

Planning the First Steps to Better Listening

To become more than a passive listener, you must follow a few steps that will enable you to become a more conscious interactive communicator. You must:

- Learn the art of disengagement, which requires you to disengage from self-concerns and concentrate on the task of gathering accurate information;

- Master the uncommon art of listening for consequences to locate a possible hidden communication;

- Develop an awareness of personal emotional reactions by determining how you feel as you listen;

- Develop an ear for patterns as well as for single, sharp responses or behaviors;

- Learn to discriminate between pertinent information and any contrived or manufactured diversions; and

- Have an understanding of the overriding function of compromise.

Rather than trying to apply the above techniques step-by-step, the listener must make them a continuous part of the communication process.

Listening Behaviors to Avoid or Implement

Usually, understanding what you are doing to make listening harder is enough to start you on the path to obtaining better listening skills. By being aware of our listening attitudes, we can turn to more productive methods of communication.

Listening Behaviors To Implement

• **Listen for Ideas and Concepts, Not Just Facts**. In other words, don't ignore the forest for the trees. Chances are that the speaker is not just conveying a list of facts. There is a reason for the communication. Look for it.

• **Force Yourself to Listen to Ideas and Subject Areas You Normally Would Avoid**. Try to listen with objectivity. Eventually, it will become easier to do.

• **Take Notes**. Note-taking helps you focus on what is being said, although it does not replace the need for attentive listening. It also enables you to make responses to certain points afterward for clarification.

• **Give Feedback and Verify What You Have Heard With the Speaker.** This should be done especially if you feel confusion or that your mind wandered during the discussion. In addition to helping you make sure you have listened well enough, it gives clues to the other person as to whether or not you properly understood the message.

- **Reconcile Thought Speed with Speech Speed**. Because people think faster than they speak, this can be a major barrier. But trying to concentrate when you feel your mind about to wander will help. Use the extra thought time to think about the speaker's message – note nonverbal behavior, antici- pate points, mentally summarize what has been said, and look for hidden meanings.

- **Be Prepared to Listen**. Before the speaker begins, prepare yourself for the interaction by motivating yourself to listen well. If you expect to hear really important information, be prepared to take notes. If it is a pleasur- able situation, be prepared to be receptive and have fun.

Listening Behaviors To Avoid

- **Don't Interrupt**. Sometimes, not interrupt- ing can be difficult, because the speaker might be the type who gives nonverbal cues indicating that he is finished, but then remembers something else he would like to say. One skill for avoiding inadvertent inter- ruption is to be on the lookout for certain words that indicate the speaker may have more to say, such as "and," "also," "besides," "because," "for example," "in other words," *etc.*

- **Don't Jump to Conclusions**. Let the speaker finish what he has to say before you decide you know what it is. Although you may have an idea of the direction the speaker is heading, wait and see if that is where he ends up before making any conclusions.

- **Don't Make Judgments**. Don't form pre-conceptions about the speaker, the subject, or the contents of the communication before you have listened.

- **Don't Become Emotional or Challenging**. Even if the speaker displays these tactics, you are better off waiting until all the data is in before responding. You may consider making one-word notes so that you don't forget what points you would like to make when it is your turn to speak.

- **Don't Let the Speaker's Delivery Stop You from Listening.** Many poor listeners use this as an excuse to not listen – but just because the sender is not an accomplished speaker does not mean that the message is worthless. It is the message that is important, not the way it is transmitted.

- **Don't Fake Attention**. This is a skill most of us mastered at an early age – pretending to listen when, in fact, we aren't paying a bit of attention to the speaker.

- **Don't Allow Distractions to Stop You From Listening**. Poor listeners often welcome any excuse that allows them to avoid listening, whereas a good listener actively fights distraction and makes the best of a bad listening circumstance. Practicing concentration can help you overcome this problem.

Chapter Three Summary

Becoming a good, empathetic listener requires more than just a good set of ear drums. It requires your active, interested involvement in all interactions – not just those in which you feel you have a personal stake. It also involves observation that lets you know the overall message, not just that imparted by specific words and tones. The nonverbal aspect of communication will be detailed further in the next chapter.

Key elements to remember from Chapter Three include:

√   Focusing on finding a solution can sometimes actually be detrimental to the service goal, because it can lead to a failure to listen. Many times, the customer's need to vent his frustrations outweighs the need to get a problem fixed.

√   Most people think they are good listeners when, in fact, they are not. Don't make that mistake. Take a close look at yourself and figure out what your blind spots are.

√   Listening is more than just the physical act of hearing – it is a communication process that requires practice and attention in order to be done effectively on a consistent basis.

√   Although 80 percent of what we learn comes from listening, the average person only retains 25 percent of the things he hears. The person with excellent listening skills will make better decisions, because he will usually have more information to work with.

√   Never, ever take things personally.

√   Remember that you are doing this for your own health, safety, well-being, and future.

CHAPTER FOUR

Behavior:
The Foundation of
Successful Service

*"It requires a very unusual mind to undertake
the analysis of the obvious."*

– Alfred North Whitehead

What Does Communication Have to Do With Service?

Have you ever had a really bad day? The kind of day where things go from mediocre to bad to worse? You may not realize it, but your attitude might be the real problem. We don't have to say anything to anybody to communicate with them. And, when we transmit negative emotions to others, whether it be by tone of voice, body posture, an unpleasant facial expression, or just a raising of eyebrows, we often find those negative emotions reflected back at us. An occurrence that, inevitably, only makes things worse.

Because the public has such a low starting opinion of service providers in general, particularly when problems with a product or service arise, it doesn't take much to push an interaction into a downward spiral of negativism. If your job is to handle complaints on a regular basis, you *must* learn how to communicate in a way designed to prevent this from happening. If you don't learn to control the interactions you have with the public, it will cause more than just your performance to suffer. Your overall attitude on a personal level will likely erode, damaging relationships in and out of the workplace, and you will probably become desperately unhappy in your job.

Managing Ourselves Before We Manage Others

The good news is it doesn't take very much effort to prevent a negative situation. Just remember that you must first manage yourself before you can possibly hope to be effective in managing anybody else. Some members of the public may simply enjoy ranting, and you already know that the way to manage them is to attentively listen before trying to address the underlying problem. But the large majority of people you will interact with are looking to you for assistance. They need your help. For this reason, most people will subconsciously look at your behavior for cues on how they should act. If you are negative, you are only promoting that sort of an interaction. And, if you are positive, you will promote similar behaviors in the other. If you display credibility and are likable, you will be the master of your service objectives.

Why are Your Verbal and Nonverbal Behaviors 'Keys' to the Solution?

Your body, your tone of voice, and the words you choose are all indicative of how you feel about things, and these are all cues that other people can read and interpret. Although we all try to hide things when we choose our words, particularly in touchy situations, cues "leak" out to reveal what we are truly feeling. This is because a lie is an unnatural thing, and the body tries to tell the truth, reacting before our conscious minds have a chance to suppress it. There may be a very good reason for a person to conceal his emotions or initial reaction to something, but he cannot stop the split-second, instinctive physical reaction.

Actually, people are fairly adept at detecting these nonverbal reactions, even if they are not consciously aware of it, and even if they are not as good at interpreting them as they think. "Hunches" and "bad feelings" are often the result of cues that people are not even aware they picked up. When given conflicting verbal and nonverbal cues, people typically believe the nonverbal ones, because their experiences have told them that these are the most reliable.

Why People Get the Wrong Impressions

Unfortunately, this leads to many people being judged unfairly. It is extremely easy for a person who is being perfectly honest to be perceived as dishonest or as hiding something. When people see that the verbal and nonverbal cues a person is using do not match, they put less faith in the verbal message. Frequently, however, the lack of congruence is caused by other factors of which the interpreter is unaware.

The following lists some of the reasons why this happens:

• **Ambiguity** – If a person is asked his opinion

on something, and he really doesn't know or can truly see both sides of an issue, he may express opposing cues in his verbal and non-verbal demeanors.

- **Qualifications** – A person may say something that he has qualifications or reservations about. These reservations might result in behaviors that can easily be misinterpreted as deception.

- **Outside Factors** – Other things can also impact congruency. For example, a person may really like someone, but be uncomfortable with something about that person. One illustration of this is a person who is allergic to another's perfume. He might smile, laugh, and talk with her in a friendly manner while trying to stay out of range of the scent.

The best way to avoid displaying this inconsistent behavior is to focus on a clear outcome, be careful to say what you mean, pay attention to nonverbal cues, avoid indicators of deception, and recognize inconsistent behavior when it occurs and work to eliminate it.

Why Does Communication Backfire So Drastically?

When we communicate with other people, even those we have known for a long time, we often assume they understand what we are trying to impart. In actuality, it is safer to assume the other does not clearly understand what we are trying to say. Just because we see things one way does not mean that others, even those with similar life experiences and backgrounds, will see them the same way. Children don't understand their parents, and parents don't understand their children, even when they are together for most of their lives. Everyone has a unique perception of the surrounding world, and an understanding of this truth can help when trying to communicate an important message to others.

It is possible for two people who see the same thing to perceive entirely different meanings. This happens because of the differences people have in their experiences, attitudes, beliefs, and backgrounds, but it is also because people are selective in what they notice. For example, one person may have been so enthralled with a bug he saw crawling on the wall that he paid scant attention to the show, while the other may have been very caught up in the program. Afterward, the first might decide the show was boring because it couldn't hold his attention, and the second person would be amazed at that perception.

Another interesting thing to note about communication is that, although the senses of touch, sight, hearing, taste, and smell are usually active, people are selective about paying attention to those senses. For example, when a person sits in a crowded room for a short time, he may only see a few things and later have only a vague impression of what the room was like. But, if he is bored and sitting in the room for a longer period of time, he is likely to perceive more, because he will be paying attention to his senses. While in the first instance he may have had only a perception of feeling overcrowded in a hot and noisy room, in the second instance he may have noted things about the people around him or the smell of the bakery down the hall.

Once you are more aware of your perceptions, you can learn to interpret them in a more meaningful way and begin to understand that what you think you saw or heard isn't necessarily what happened. There are several reasons why our perceptions differ so dramatically from those of others:

- **Physical Reasons** – Every human body is different. Two people standing side-by-side may have differing interpretations of something simply because one person cannot hear as well as the other. Other physical factors such as seating in a similar circumstance may play a role. For example, a person with orchestra seats at the theater may respond better emotionally to a musical than a person with seats at the rear of the upper balcony.

- **Knowledge and Experience** – One person's education level or background may give him an advantage in understanding something, whereas another might not understand certain references because his education level or background is different.

- **Individual Circumstances** – A person's mood may impact how he feels about something. Even the time of day may make a difference, because a person who is tired often has less of an ability to perceive than a person who is just beginning his day.

- **Expectations** – If we "expect" something, we often will tune our perceptions to coincide with that expectation. For example, if a parent goes to a parent-teacher conference expecting to hear good things about his child, he may have a difficult time understanding what the teacher is trying to say if he or she is not saying what the parent expected to hear.

- **Interpretation** – We all interpret things in a unique way. We may focus on one thing, and then classify the items around it in relation to the one thing. Others, however, may focus on another thing and classify the surrounding objects in relation to it. Therefore, we may come up with completely different interpretations of the same thing. When witnessing an event where many things happen at once, one person might focus on one happening and classify any subsequent actions in relation to the original event he or she noticed. Another person, however, might have noted a different occurrence first, and the overall outcome might take on a different meaning than it did for the first person.

The Skilled Art of Verbal Communication

The words you choose when interacting with the public are extremely important, as is the way you use those words. In essence, you can use them as either a tool or a weapon. A wrong word can stir up resentment and set up a communication barrier, even if you didn't mean what you said in a negative way.

The use of words in communication has much more to do with how we perceive things than the mere meaning of the words alone. How we pronounce words, the tone of voice in which they are uttered, word choice – each of these is a factor in the communication process.

Increase your vocabulary so that you can use words to express the same ideas in different ways. A salesperson with a gifted vocabulary, for example, can learn to describe his product in many different ways designed to motivate the customer into buying the product. Use expressive words in a positive manner. Words such as "exclusive" or "spectacular" create positive images, for example. Dynamic words such as "provocative" and "vibrant" are designed to excite people about things. Words such as "I," "you," "we," and "our" are personal words you can use to help build relationships with your customers or cause them to relate something to themselves (such as the product or service). Get a thesaurus and practice integrating new descriptive words into your vocabulary. Make a game out of it – have fun.

Analyze your word choices and speaking behaviors. Try to figure out how they appear to other people. Pay attention to how others come across. Are they effective? Could they be doing something better? Are there things about them you can emulate? The following are some things to look for:

- **Greeting Rituals** – Try to sound like you care when you greet the customer for the first time. Don't use monotones or sound like you are reading a too-well-rehearsed script.

- **Enunciation** – Make sure you are speaking clearly. Use pauses and match the speech rate of the other person.

- **Vocal Tones** – Make sure they are pleasant and match what you are trying to say.

- **Interruptions** – Don't do it. You don't like it, and neither does anyone else.

- **Exaggeration** – If you are promoting a product or service, avoid the temptation to exaggerate its qualities. Tell the truth.

- **Congruency** – Your facial expressions and body language should reflect how you feel and should match what you are trying to express through your words.

- **Cultivate Your Memory** – Learn the tricks of remembering people's names. Repeat them; write them down. People like to be remembered.

- **Closing Rituals** – Learn to say goodbye in a conversational style. As with greeting rituals, you don't want to sound scripted. It implies that you don't really care and could negatively impact future relations with that person. Try to make your customers leave with the feeling that you really were glad to talk to them.

Things to Say/Never Say When Dealing with Complainants

The following are guidelines to use for becoming a better verbal communicator in service circumstances.

Verbal Behaviors to Practice

- **Recognize the Differences Between Facts, Reports, and Inferences** – You must learn to separate these in order to avoid reaching the wrong conclusions. Facts are the actual events or bits of information. When we report the facts, however, we tell them in the way we perceive them – which may distort them somewhat. No two people perceive things in the same way. People often infer things from these reports and make judgments about them. However, it is easy to infer the wrong thing. If someone says "Dr. Thomas," for example, it may be inferred that Dr. Thomas is a medical doctor. In reality, however, Dr. Thomas may have a Ph.D. in business. The inference is incorrect.

- **Be Positive** – Words can be used in a way which illustrates positive aspects or negative aspects, even when the intent of the service provider is to be positive. For example, saying, "it isn't as bad as it could be," is actually a negative statement, because it is still showing that something is wrong. It is better to focus on the ease of fixing the problem. For example, it's not a "serious problem," it's a "different situation."

- **Give the Customer as Much Time As He**

or She Needs – Don't be in a rush. Make sure you have answered all the customer's concerns. Trying to rush a client is often self-defeating, only making the problem worse and making him even angrier. Even if you know how to fix the problem already, allow him as much time as he needs. Let the customer decide when the interaction is over.

- **Be Prepared to Handle Long-Winded Customers With Diplomacy** – There is often a reason for a customer to stay in contact after you have helped him with his problem. He may not understand your explanation of how to fix the problem, or he may not be satisfied with the resolution. He may just be lonely and want somebody to talk to. Handle the situation with diplomacy, and ask questions designed to see if any clarification is needed or if there are further problems you can help with. Example of a diplomatic close: "Well, if you don't have any more questions, it looks like you're all set. Give me a call if you have any other questions or if something unexpected comes up that I can help you with."

Verbal Behaviors to Avoid

- **Avoid Placing Blame** – Don't say things like, "I think you were wrong." This seems to focus blame on the other person, and that causes an immediate defensive response. A better method would be to say something like, "I could be wrong, but didn't the program say the event was tomorrow?"

Using Words More Effectively

Wrong	*Right*
Don't forget . . .	– Please remember . . .
Give me . . .	– Can you . . .
I can't . . .	– My supervisor can . . .
I hate to say it, but . . .	– The warranty has expired, but this is what we can do . . .
I know this will work . .	– I'm confident in this procedure . . .
I want . . .	– Could you please . . .
I'm sorry . . .	– Thank you for . . .
It isn't so bad . . .	– We can fix this easily . . .
Serious problem . . .	– Different situation . . .
Tell me . . .	– Would you please describe . . .
What do you want?	– How can I help you?
You broke it . . .	– It works best when . . .
You have a problem . . .	– I can help you . . .
You have to . . .	– I would appreciate it if . . .
Your problem . . .	– We need to . . .
Your problem . . .	– This situation . . .
You're wrong . . .	– I may be incorrect, but . . .

- **Don't Express Your Opinions** – When you express an opinion, it weakens your position. If you tell a customer you agree with him that the product is a piece of junk, all you are doing is reaffirming his suspicions that your company isn't any good, and this will make your job more difficult.

- **Never Make Promises You Can't Keep** – You can never be sure that your product or service will last forever, and your customer

knows it. It will decrease his confidence in
you if you make unrealistic guarantees.

- **Don't Make Demands** – Phrase things so
that they are requests rather than requirements. Instead of saying, "Give me your
address so I can send you the part," say "Can
I get your address? I need to mail you the
part."

- **Don't React to Negative Behaviors** – No
matter how provoked you become, don't
allow yourself to respond to the other with
similar behaviors. If the customer uses vulgar language, refrain from using it yourself.
Remember that your behaviors can encourage the other to modify his to a similar manner. If you respond to the customer by acting
negatively, it can only escalate the situation.
You don't need that.

The Art of Nonverbal Communication

Your nonverbal behaviors tell others whether you are reliable, honest, and open. But do you know what your body is saying
when you aren't paying attention?

There are three basic behavioral dimensions that people display when they interact with others. These are credibility, interpersonal attractiveness (or likability), and dominance. We use individual
behaviors to stress these image dimensions depending on our goals.
Supervisors and employers tend to stress the images of dominance,
successful politicians stress their credibility, and entertainers stress
their interpersonal attractiveness.

Usually, we balance these image dimensions to meet our
needs. The employer must be dominant, but he also must be perceived as credible and likable to at least a certain extent. The politi-

cian must be credible, but he must also be likable in order to get votes. And people want him to be able to display dominance when the situation requires it.

But it is not easy to balance these dimensions. Emphasizing one type of image correspondingly decreases another dimension. For example, the person who displays many dominance cues is correspondingly less likable.

As a service provider, you need to be both credible and likable. Your service objective will determine which of the two you need to emphasize and which is secondary. The image dimension of dominance is self-defeating in service situations, because it can only anger those you interact with.

Nonverbal Behaviors
to Implement or Avoid

In public service, there are certain behaviors that are more effective than others. Some can damage your credibility and likability before you even open your mouth. The following behavioral management strategies tell you which behaviors to cultivate and which behaviors to avoid when interacting with others.

Things To Do To Increase Credibility

•   Your behaviors should be consistent, and

your verbal and nonverbal messages should match.

- Don't address your client in an overly formal manner. To be seen as more credible and likable, treat the customer in a more familiar, casual manner.

- If you meet the public in a face-to-face setting, make sure your clothing and personal appearance match what the public expects.

- Your posture should be relaxed and confident.

- When you lean towards another person, it illustrates that you are interested in what that person has to say.

- When interacting with others, use natural facial expressions and sincere smiles.

- Your smiles should be made at appropriate times during the course of the conversation. Avoid smiling excessively. People perceive this as insincere.

- Maintain high levels of relaxed and confident eye contact, but it shouldn't be continuous or challenging.

- The safest way to break eye contact is by looking downward.

- Your gestures and movements should be relaxed and confident.

- Use gestures more often – this makes you

seem more sincere than you would look with a stiff or nonmoving appearance.

* Use relaxed, natural tones when speaking to others.

* People who use a relatively fast speaking rate with an appropriate volume are generally considered more credible than those who seem deliberately slow.

* Use short pauses during the course of your conversation.

* If you have an accent that differs significantly from the typical person you serve, realize that a barrier is present and attempt to conform to the standard accent or learn to compensate so that the barrier is minimized. Learn to recognize situations where your accent is a problem for your client.

* Avoid terms such as "um," "er," "sort of," "oh, well," and "like."

How To Make Yourself More Likable

* Reduce the barriers to communication. Don't allow anything to come between you and visual contact with your client.

* When interacting face-to-face with someone, be sure to use a close but appropriate distance. Be careful not to violate the other's personal space. If the other moves away from you, allow him to set the proper interaction distance.

- When you show you are interested in the other person, you are more likable. You can show interest with direct body and head orientation, leaning forward or towards the other, and displaying a relaxed body with open postures.

- Research studies show that people who are physically attractive are generally better-liked. Make sure your clothing meets the expectations of your public.

- Be spontaneous, and cultivate nonverbal behaviors which are open and disclosing.

- Use your face – a high amount of expressiveness will make you more likable. Pleasant facial expressions are, of course, preferable.

- Be responsive with your behaviors, using smiles, nodding your head, shrugging, or otherwise showing that you are attending to the other person. If you are talking to someone on the phone, you would do this in the form of verbal responses ("yes," "uh huh," "I agree," *etc.*).

- Smile a lot, but make sure that your smiles are in context and sincere. Avoid excessive smiling.

- You should employ a good degree of direct and attentive eye contact, sustaining it for moderate to high periods of time.

- Maintain a mutual gaze with the person you are interacting with.

- Move your body – change posture and gesture frequently in response to the other person.

- Use open behaviors to show your interest and openness to what the person is telling you. For instance, you might use open hand positions, such as hands resting in the lap.

- Give positive vocal reinforcement in the form of such terms as "yes," "uh huh," or "you're right."

- Your voice should be warm and relaxed, yet expressive, dynamic, and animated. Your voice should be confident, friendly, and pleasant. Be sure to use your voice to express your interest in the other person.

- Your laughter should be genuine and appropriate. Avoid false, insincere laughter.

- Lighter-colored, informal clothing increases likability.

Behaviors Service Personnel Should Avoid

- Don't display inconsistent verbal and nonverbal messages.

- Low levels of nonverbal behavior are to be avoided. Don't blatantly plan or censor your movements.

- Avoid any nonverbal behaviors which make you appear to be secretive.

- Don't dress in a manner that is too informal or too formal – meet the expectations of the public you are likely to encounter.

- A lack of facial expressiveness or hiding your expressions should be avoided. Avoid using unpleasant facial expressions.

- Lowered-brow positions are frequently used in expressing anger, so these expressions tend to be perceived as negative.

Behavior and the Seven Steps of Positive Service

1. **Mental Preparation** – Approach the interaction positively.

   MAJOR BEHAVIORS: Interested, respectful, friendly, likable.

2. **Listen** – Be patient. Look for hidden and unspoken meanings.

   MAJOR BEHAVIORS: Interested, respectful, concerned.

3. **Respond** – Ask questions and give feedback.

   MAJOR BEHAVIORS: Concerned, helpful, respectful.

4. **Understand** – Use the given information to assess the whole problem, which may be more than the customer

- People who don't smile or smile infrequent-ly are less trusted.

- Insincere smiles, or smiles that seem to be out of context can make you appear to be less credible and less likable. Many people are unaware that their insincerity shows.

- The lack of visual attention causes a person to be less likable, because he seems to be disinterested.

first revealed.

MAJOR BEHAVIORS: Respectful, professional.

5. **Assist** – Fix the problem if possible. Do what you can do for the customer.

MAJOR BEHAVIORS: Concerned, helpful, truthful, professional, empa-thetic.

6. **Verify** – Make sure the customer understands the instructions for fixing a problem and that all his concerns are addressed as fully as possible.

MAJOR BEHAVIORS: Concerned, listening, respectful.

7. **Conclude** – Finish the interaction without rushing.

MAJOR BEHAVIORS: Respectful, friendly, patient.

- Avoid challenging or prolonged eye contact. Don't stare.

- Don't use high levels of eye contact while speaking followed by low levels of eye contact while listening.

- Continuously looking down, averting gaze, or using generally low levels of eye contact can make you seem less trustworthy.

- Avoid being the first to break eye contact, as this can make you appear to be less trustworthy.

- Looking down before responding to a question or shifting your eyes can be interpreted as deceptive, as can other nervous eye behaviors.

- Don't break eye contact in a sideways motion, it will probably be interpreted as disinterest or boredom. It's best to break contact by looking downward, except as mentioned above.

- Breaking eye contact with an upward motion has an unsettling or startling effect.

- Interrupting the other person implies that you are not interested in what he has to say. Even if your purpose is to keep the conversation on track, avoid interruptions.

- Don't allow vocal tones which suggest anger, irritation, boredom, or other negative emotions to enter your interactions.

- A tense voice can cause a negative reaction in others.

- Avoid overlapping speech when the client is speaking.

- Don't address the other in an overly formal manner.

- Avoid speaking in a non-general, regionally specific dialect because it can pose a barrier for communication. If you do speak with an accent, be careful to ensure that the other can understand you.

- Avoid using slang that others may not understand. Don't use meaningless particles such as "you know."

- Hesitating, hedging, or not being fluent in your speech can make you seem less credible.

- Avoid the lack of positive vocal reinforcement or the absence of vocal warmth. Don't use a narrow range of pitch or volume.

- Failing to laugh when appropriate is extremely negative, but so is laughter at inappropriate times. False or phony laughter is to be avoided.

- Avoid closed body postures, such as hugging your body or crossing your arms across your chest.

- Indirect postures, such as turning the trunk of the body or your face away from the other, can be perceived as negative or deceptive. A decrease or lack of forward leans can be perceived as disinterest.

- A tense posture should be avoided – appear relaxed.

- Don't use an overly close interpersonal distance – if the other is uncomfortable with how close you are standing, allow him to set the proper distance.

- Avoid allowing barriers to come between you and the other. Barriers can be a desk, for instance, or a plant or computer that blocks the visual line of sight.

- Don't "swoop down" on a client as he enters the room. Be courteous and interested, and give the customer your immediate attention but avoid being "too much."

- Avoid nervous behaviors such as wringing your hands or moistening your lips.

- Don't click your pen on and off or rattle coins in your pocket. Notice if the customer does these things – it could be signaling unease or impatience.

- Avoid tapping your fingers. This tells the other that you are impatient.

- Gestures or overall body movements which appear to be tense or nervous are harmful, as is an absence of gestures or body movement.

- Avoid the absence of responsive behaviors

such as head-nodding.

- Don't overtly hurry people with your behaviors. Use gestures to give subtle signals, however. For instance, to signify your readiness to end an interaction, simple gestures such as putting a cap on a pen and putting it in your pocket or straightening your desk or work area can be helpful without being obvious. The customer may not be consciously aware of the signal, but he may respond to it nonetheless.

- Closed hand positions, such as folding them under crossed arms or clenching the fist, are negative behaviors.

- In general, avoid physically touching customers, because such contact can be so widely misinterpreted or considered to be offensive.

Taking a Closer Look at Your Body's Language

The following pages show illustrations of some of the basic human emotions and behaviors service personnel and the public encounter on a daily basis. These illustrative photographs were used with permission from the book, *The Power of Impression Management*, by Dr. Donald Slowik and Cara Cantarella (1998). While examining these photos, take a step back and consider how you would feel if you encountered someone with these expressions and emotions. How would you feel if you were a customer and you met a service provider displaying these emotions? As a service provider, how would you cope with a customer showing these behaviors?

ATTENTION

These photographs illustrate body language that can be translated as indicating levels of an individual's interest and attention in a communication exchange. In general, behavior characteristics associated with high interest are:

- Forward lean
- One or both legs drawn back
- Open body language
- Hands still and relaxed
- Attentive facial expression
- Eyes focused and attentive

INTEREST

Interest: The feeling of one whose attention, concern, or curiosity is particularly engaged by something, someone, or some event. Interest is evident in the way people attend to one another. It almost always involves a direct gaze that unmistakably illustrates that one person has another's complete attention.

- Slightly raised eyebrows
- Direct gaze
- Bright eyes
- Dilated pupils
- Corners of the mouth may be upturned

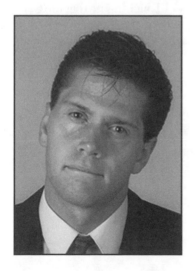

LIKING

Another set of attitudes which can be diagnosed through assessment of body language concerns the level of "liking" or interest which a person displays in another. The photographs depicted show people whose body language reveals a high degree of liking or interest in the other. Note the following indicators displayed:

- Smiling (genuine)
- Open-body position and gestures
- Leaning towards the other
- Directly facing the other
- Affirmative head-nodding
- Closeness to the other
- Touching or reaching out
- Direct eye contact
- Mirrored or matched positions
- Relaxed body
- Enthusiastic expression

BEWILDERMENT

Bewilderment: A state or quality of feeling confused or completely puzzled; perplexed. Bewilderment is a universal emotion and a communication tool cultivated to inform others that we do not understand what is happening or what is being said.

- Eyebrows furrowed, drawn down over eyes
- Wrinkled forehead
- Head leaned forward
- Opened mouth, with dropped lower jaw

TRUTHFULNESS

Photographic depictions of "truthfulness" are presented here. Note that each of the individuals pictured displays one or more of the following characteristics:

- True, "felt happy" smile
- Direct eye contact
- Clear, confident eyes
- Confident, erect posture
- Sense of being at ease
- Relaxed responses
- Appropriate movements

DEFENSIVENESS

There are two types of defensiveness – aggressive defensiveness and protective defensiveness. The individual who displays a protective defense to a perceived attack will put up physical barriers designed to protect himself and shield him from perceived threats. These barriers, as pictured at right, may involve:

- Closed arms
- Closed body posture
- Crossed legs
- Leaning back or away from perceived attack
- Averted gaze, lack of eye contact

The display of an aggressive defense is offensive in nature. The person who responds aggressively to a perceived attack desires to retaliate in a forceful manner. This individual may display the following behaviors:

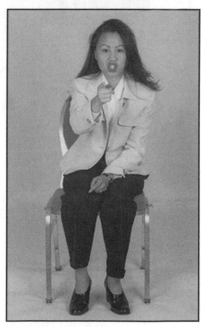

- Leaning forward
- Feet planted firmly on floor, spaced apart
- Direct eye contact
- Closed body

ANGER

Anger: A strong feeling of displeasure and belligerence aroused by a real or supposed wrong; an experience of sudden displeasure accompanied by an impulse to retaliate. Anger is visible in the overall facial expression, from eye behaviors to lines on the face to the shape of the mouth.

- Clenched teeth
- Pressed lips
- Less-pronounced cheek lines from nose to mouth
- Direct, solid stare
- Brows drawn down over eyes
- Wrinkled forehead
- Pinched area between brows

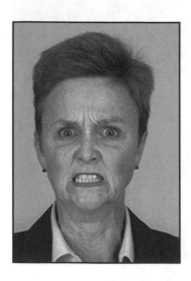

DISINTEREST/BOREDOM

The following pictures demonstrate disinterest or boredom. Behaviors associated with disinterest include:

- Leaning back
- Dropping the head
- Supporting the head in one hand
- Closed gestures
- Crossed arms and legs
- Shoulders slouched
- Non-enthusiastic facial expressions
- Diverted or unfocused eyes

DISGUST

Disgust: A state or quality of feeling repugnance caused by something offensive; strong aversion; impatient dissatisfaction; to cause nausea or loathing in. People who are disgusted usually reveal their emotion most distinctively in the lower portion of their faces – as illustrated below.

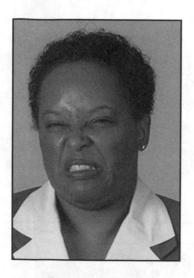

- Lips curled
- Upper lip drawn back on one side
- Eyebrows furrowed
- Eyebrows pulled down over eyes
- Crinkling in bridge of nose
- One nostril slightly flared

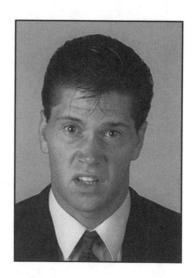

DISLIKING

These photographs each show an individual displaying a high degree of dislike for or disinterest in another. Each person depicted in these photographs utilizes closed gestures to show lack of connection and dislike. Several key indicators are displayed:

- Averted eyes/limited eye contact
- Furrowed eyebrows
- Rigid body
- Closed bodily stance
- Arms and legs crossed
- Body tension and rigidity
- Disinterested expression
- Unpleasant expression
- Resistant body language
- Tight-lipped expression
- Tense jaw line

CONTEMPT

Contempt: A feeling with which one regards anything considered mean, vile, or worthless; disdain; scorn; a willful disobedience to, or open disrespect for, rules or orders. Flared nostrils, a tight jaw line, and narrowed eyes are the key indicators people give when experiencing the universal emotion of contempt.

- Narrowed eyes
- Flared nostrils
- Slightly squinted eyes
- Tight jaw line
- Lips pressed together
- Lips possibly turned up at one corner

CONCEALMENT

An individual who is concealing information may also display characteristic behaviors, as depicted in the following photographs. When individuals withhold or hide information, they may display this "hiding" behavior with hand gestures, either covering their mouths with a hand or hiding their faces with a hand.

Chapter Four Summary

Your word choices and your body's nonverbal reactions are continuously giving messages to other people that you can't afford to have misinterpreted. The best service providers are both credible and likable. To convey these qualities, you need to make sure that your verbal and nonverbal cues are working harmoniously. You can't afford for your words to say one thing while your body tells observers something else.

Once you have these aspects of communication under control, you can handle virtually any public service situation, including those circumstances involving difficult or angry customers. More information about how to deal with this type of complaint is presented in Chapter Six.

Key elements to remember from Chapter Four include:

√   Learn to recognize how your attitude can impact the success or failure of your interactions with others. You must first manage yourself before you can possibly hope to be effective in managing anybody else.

√   No matter how hard we try to hide things when we choose our words, cues "leak" out to reveal what we are truly feeling.

√   Sometimes, our body will give contradictory messages even when we are being honest with the words we choose and the messages we are giving verbally.

√   Learn to choose words that are positive and avoid placing blame. Even if you don't intend things negatively, certain words cause people to react defensively.

√   Good service providers show themselves to be both credible and likable. There are specific behaviors you can use to enhance these image dimensions.

√   Never, ever take things personally.

√   Remember that you are doing this for your own health, safety, well-being, and future.

CHAPTER FIVE

Maintaining Customer Service During Negotiation

*"All government – indeed, every human benefit
and enjoyment, every virtue and every prudent act –
is founded on compromise and barter."*

Edmund Burke, Philosopher. 1729-1797.

Why Does Negotiation Present Such a Challenge to the Service
   Provider?
How Can You Negotiate and Be Honest at the Same Time?
How Can You Be Persuasive Yet Still Provide Adequate Service?
Why Must You Worry So Much About the Customer's Needs?
How Do You Prepare for a Negotiation?
How is Negotiation a Controlled Conflict?
Are You Using Behavior Management During Negotiations?
What are the Tools of Negotiation?
What Things Should You Avoid When Negotiating?
What Should You Do if You Make a Mistake During Negotiations?
What Should You Do if the Negotiation Fails?

Why Does Negotiation Present Such a Challenge to the Service Provider?

Imagine going to buy a new car. You do your research and find out how much you should pay. You understand how much each option you choose should add to the price. You know how much the model you desire should cost you while still giving a fair profit to the dealer.

Now imagine how you would feel if the dealer tries to overcharge you several thousand dollars even after you show him your figures. Will you feel respected? Or will you feel insulted about the dealer's judgment of your intelligence?

Imagine interrupting your busy schedule only to have a salesperson keep you waiting for hours while he completes tasks you later realize were only invented so that you wouldn't be willing to waste the time investment by walking away from the sale.

Suppose you eventually settle on a price and leave the car so that additional options can be installed. How will you feel if your subsequent phone calls to see if the vehicle is ready are not returned? Will you feel like your business is appreciated?

You've just spent thousands of dollars on one item, and you can't get the attention of the salesperson. You can't even get him to return your phone calls. Are you ever going to shop at that dealership again? Obviously not. Yet these types of tactics are repeatedly used during negotiated sales on a daily basis.

If your profits are based on the prices you garner in negotiated sales, you must strike a precarious balance between satisfying your customer and making a fair profit. Every sale you handle is potentially damaging for yourself and your organization. You may make the sale you are working on, but you could prevent several future sales.

If your customer returns to his home or office and starts brooding over the tactics used against him, your future profitability and reputation could suffer. If the customer feels mistreated or cheated, he will probably tell anybody and everybody who asks just exactly what he thinks about your company and its tactics.

Negotiation with integrity is a challenge – yet it is a challenge that is legitimately managed by the best sales people on a daily basis. You don't have to be dishonest to make negotiated sales, and you don't have to use unfair or unreasonable tactics to make your sales. Treat the public or your customers the way you would want to be treated in similar circumstances.

How Can You Negotiate and Be Honest at the Same Time?

Perhaps you should ask how can you negotiate a sale without being honest. In today's legal environment, neither you nor your organization can afford to be dishonest with your customers. Not only is there a legal liability issue, but a positive working environment encourages satisfactory employer-employee relationships, and it reduces the stress level of employees if only by minimizing confrontational situations between customers and employees.

While there is an element of deception inherent in any negotiation process, you should treat it more as a theatrical process than as a dishonest one. If you sell used cars and you clean them up to a beautiful shine to try and attract attention to them, you are merely presenting your products in the most effective fashion. You are not lying – your customer is well aware of what you are doing and does not object. This, too, is what you are doing when you honestly negotiate sales of your products and services.

Your customers want to be treated with respect. They want you to listen to them and answer their concerns confidently and quickly. They want you to be honest when you answer the questions they will naturally have about your product or service. They expect you to present it in the best light, and they expect you to try and get a fair price.

How Can You Be Persuasive Yet Still Provide Adequate Service?

You won't fully satisfy your customers without being honest, but that doesn't mean there are no techniques you can use to sell products or services. There are several sales strategies that every customer service provider should be aware of, even when sales are not your primary task in your organization.

- Attract the attention of your company's potential customers. Your organization will probably accomplish much of this task for you through advertising, glitzy packaging, and so on.

- Ask questions – your customers will tell you what they want if you give them the opportunity to do so. You can then use this information to match the customer to the products or services he or she is most likely to desire or need.

- Tell the customer what is good about the products or services you are trying to sell to him. Show the product off. Describe the benefits.

- Reflect the customer's desires. Show the customer that you understand what he or she is saying by paraphrasing the customer's comments or restating them.

- Let the customer set the sales style you use during the negotiation process. Some people like to make up their own minds while others want you to tell them everything there is to know about the product or service. Some people make their decisions quickly based on solid facts, while others are slow to choose. Some will buy quickly based on their emotions, while others want time to think about it and talk it over with their friends or members of their family. Adjust to each person individually.

- Find out what the customer considers to be the primary selling features of your product or service. Emphasize these features in order to make your sales.

- Resolve the customer's concerns. Find out what they are and carefully prove them to be insignificant or show how other features minimize them.

- Suggest additional products and services. You may make additional sales and improve the customer's satisfaction with these recommendations.

- Learn to accept rejection. A customer may have many reasons for refusing to accept your offer. Never take it personally. Learn from your mistakes and continue on. Try to avoid letting rejection damage your self-esteem or your relationships with future customers.

Why Must You Worry So Much About the Customer's Needs?

You cannot be successful in your sales unless you meet the customer's needs. Frequently, negotiators tend to concentrate on sealing the bargain to the exclusion of other factors. They may be enthusiastic and eloquent about their products, and they may be able to tell their potential customers everything about the subject – but if it doesn't meet the customer's needs or desires, the sale will not be successful.

Even if a client comes to you already intent on purchasing the product, you should attempt to open a dialogue about that product to make sure that the customer truly will have his needs met with that product. There may be a more suitable product available. While the sale is important, future customer relations should also be considered. Will an unhappy customer come back? What will he tell others about the product or service? There are many factors that can prevent or stop a sale from occurring.

Some of the most common factors that prevent a sale from taking place include:

- **Wrong market** – If the marketing efforts are aimed at the wrong audience, you are unlikely to be successful. While you might achieve a sale now and then, this will likely be due to luck rather than a sound marketing strategy.

- **Varied circumstances** – Being from different backgrounds or concentrating on different concerns can make it difficult for two people to reach an understanding. This tendency of human nature can be overcome if you try to understand the other person's point of view.

- **Personality conflicts** – Factors such as social standing or education can influence our personalities and cause us to "clash" with others of different backgrounds and personalities. To overcome this, you must consider the situation in light of the customer's point of view and attempt to communicate with him at his own level.

- **Poor presentation** – You must learn to provide an organized presentation about your product or service while still being able to tailor the information to fit the needs of the client.

- **Too little or too much information** – Some customers want a lot of detailed information about a product or service, and others do not. You should learn to adjust your approach as necessary.

- **Privacy** – Whenever possible, work in an area where distractions can be minimized. Interruptions can cause a loss of energy to the process that might not be regained, and many people demand privacy in discussing matters such as finance.

- **Poor listening** – You and your prospective customer should be involved in the communication process. This not only ensures that both sides will listen carefully, but it prevents you from unintentionally dominating the conversation and ignoring the needs of the customer.

- **Miscommunication** – You may not be making your presentation in a clear enough manner, or you may have misinterpreted the needs of the purchaser.

- **Hidden agendas** – People are not always straightforward when communicating their needs or desires. If you attempt to respond to a customer's stated needs, you will have difficulty in communicating if those goals are not the true objectives of the customer. Engaging in less formal conversation about the product or industry can help you better assess the customer's real objectives.

- **High-pressure tactics** – People don't like to be pushed into things, and service providers can sometimes be overzealous in their enthusiasm for their products. When this occurs, a client who might buy a product under other circumstances might choose to retreat from the sales process.

How Do You Prepare for a Negotiation?

Negotiation is not an art you only practice when trying to "sell" your product or service. Everybody negotiates every day – that is how we get the things we need and desire. To achieve your goals, you have to work with others – you have to have the ability to reach agreements. There are two forms of negotiation:

1.   Competitive, where the goal is to win at all costs, and

2.   Collaborative, where the goal is to ensure that both sides win.

As a service provider, you are almost certainly trying to negotiate in a collaborative fashion. While competitive tactics may win you an additional sale or two in the beginning, in the long run it will probably be detrimental to your success and that of your organization's. Usually, the collaborative process is the more efficient and effective method, because it guarantees that all persons in the negotiation process feel that their concerns were heard and understood, and that their needs will be met. In order to reach a collaborative agreement, it is necessary to understand the needs and objectives of both sides so that a solution can be identified that meets all these various imperatives.

Again, negotiation skills apply to all facets of your personal and professional life. While the emphasis here is on customer sales and other forms of workplace negotiation, the communication tools described here are applicable to all facets of your interactions with others and are particularly valuable for you if you find yourself in a conflict situation.

Negotiation is a process. It is rarely a single conversation or event. Time plays a key role in its success, but it is important to keep this in perspective. Certain things need to be accomplished during the different stages of the process. In order, a negotiator should:

1. Determine goals
2. Analyze the current situation
3. Lay the groundwork for discussion
4. Approach the other side
5. Close the deal.

In sales and service situations, many of these steps are completed before you even meet the customer. You know what your sales goals are, and your advertising or the literature about your product and service is already available to the customer. You and the customer often will already have quite a bit of the groundwork laid before you even meet.

How is Negotiation a Controlled Conflict?

Not all conflict is negative. Conflict can lead to progress in the form of friendly competition or fuel a change that can lead to success or greater productivity. Some businesses, such as professional sports, are based entirely on the creation of artificial conflict.

Many businesses find it to be an effective practice to encourage competitiveness in the workplace through incentives meant to increase the productivity, skills, and performance of workers. But, of course, not all forms of conflict are desirable and, if uncontrolled, can have quite a detrimental effect. Negative forms of conflict include:

1. **Clashing egos** – The classic power struggle is often the cause of dissension.

2. **Conflicting beliefs** – When people believe in different things and are certain that they

"are right," this can be a foundation for conflict.

3.   **Dishonesty** – In the long run, dishonesty causes far more trouble than it avoids. Unfortunately, because fraud and duplicity are pervasive in the workplace, this type of conflict is a common one.

4.   **Failure to establish boundaries** – If people don't know what another's limits are, they inevitably will step over them. This leads to resentment and, ultimately, conflict.

5.   **Fear** – A frequent cause of conflict, these fears (such as the fear of failure, fear of another person's anger, or the fear of rejection) often are unfounded.

6.   **Hidden agendas** – People are not always honest about their objectives, and unexpected problems can arise because of it.

7.   **Impatience** – People who are impatient often step on the toes of others, causing anger, resentment, and conflict.

8.   **Misdirected energy** – Sometimes, we go so far out of our way to avoid one sort of conflict that we create others.

9.   **Misunderstandings** – Miscommunication is one of the most common causes of conflicts between people.

10.   **Negligence** – Sometimes people are guilty of negligence by not carrying through with responsibilities or by forgetting promises

they've made.

11.   **Revenge motivation** – People will hold grudges even over minor things, and sometimes they have a "get even" attitude, even if they are not consciously aware of it.

Understanding the motivation of others prior to entering negotiations is a necessary part of the preliminary work you need to perform. Not every customer or client looking for a product or service has the same motivation. You will be in a stronger position to negotiate the "sale" if you understand what that person's motivation is.

Are You Using Behavior Management During Negotiations?

You cannot negotiate successfully with anyone if you cannot control your personal behaviors. This is the first step to managing the personal behaviors others display toward you. Negotiations can be an emotional process – it is a controlled conflict. How you respond to the other's tactics will put you in either a position of strength or a position of weakness.

Some common tactics you need to be prepared for include:

•   **Emotional** – The other might use a loud, angry voice or act like he or she is being taken advantage of to try to control your behavior or even force you to reconsider a position or withdraw completely from negotiations.

•   **Refusal to compromise** – With some people, concessions are considered a weakness. They may attempt to counter a proposed compromise by refusing to reciprocate or only making a very small change in their position.

- **Lack of authority** – Some, to take the pressure off themselves, may say they do not have the authority to negotiate. Or, they may say that the decision needs to be made by others.

- **Treating it like a joke** – Another tactic for defusing a negotiation is to treat the negotiation process as if it is not serious. They may make unrealistic or outrageous proposals in an attempt to put you off balance.

What are the
Tools of Negotiation?

The tactics described here can be applied throughout your negotiation process as needed. There are probably hundreds of things that a person can do while negotiating to get what he wants. But just because a technique can be effective does not mean it should be used. In fact, many techniqes may cause harm to your overall success in the long run .

Generate competition for your services – Don't consider your negotiation process in light of what you want. You will be more successful if you pay more attention to what you have to offer or sell. The more your skills and abilities or product is needed by others, the more you can get for them.

Have reasons – When you begin negotiating, you need to have reasons for what you are after, and you need to be able to articulate these reasons in a logical, reasonable way. You need to know what you are going to say before you go into a meeting with the person with whom you are in negotiation.

Good news, bad news – If you have a piece of information, demand, objective or other desire you know will be hard for the other side to swallow, try sandwiching it between pieces of good news.

Finding precedent – People tend to have an aversion to change, and sometimes have to be eased into it. Precedent can therefore work to your advantage.

"What might happen if" – If you present your needs in a way that shows consequences that might occur if these needs are not met, it will paint a clearer picture of the situation for the other side. Show the bad before the good. For example, real estate agents often show less desirable places to their customers before moving on to better properties.

Be persuasive – Once you have the facts and understand the other person's or party's position, you need to convince that person that your assertion is the correct one. To be persuasive, you must use your strengths and knowledge to:

•   Make the other side understand your position.

•   Produce evidence supporting your position.

•   Make the other side believe it should meet your needs.

Get commitment from others – In some situations, it's more effective, and less risky, to negotiate as a group (hence unions). When you can get others behind you, acting as a group, not only do you share the risks, but you increase the stakes for the other side.

Get the other side to make an investment – The easiest way to make the other side increase its stake in the negotiation process is to get them to make an investment. The more time, money, and/or energy the other side expends, the more it will want to make sure that the process reaches some sort of a successful conclusion. Time is valuable, and starting over can be expensive. If incorrectly used, this can have negative consequences in the future, however.

What Type of Person are You Dealing With?

Once you have identified the type of person you are dealing with, you can choose suitable negotiation tactics. Among the personality-types you might encounter are:

- Someone who is placating, always trying to calm things down and get things back into their "proper place" with a minimum of fuss and of change.

- The person who likes to put it all on the line and get to the meat of the problem quickly.

- Someone who tries to divert attention from the real issue. This person may suggest quick fixes that do not really address the underlying problems. (This person should not be confused with someone who simply switches to discussion on a secondary point merely to let things

Be the first to compromise – If you show a willingness to bend, it encourages similar behavior in others. It can be effective to start off by making an unexpected concession. Of course, you don't want to give away your bargaining position, nor do you want to imply that you are a pushover.

Ask for help – Sometimes, it is effective to simply come out and ask for help or state that you don't

> calm down again before returning to the primary problem.)
>
> • The negative person who believes that no new ideas will work or that they have all been tried before.
>
> • The person who passes the blame for a problem onto others.
>
> • Someone who wears a mask in an attempt to keep his feelings or opinions to himself.
>
> • The person who doesn't want to get involved and has to be coaxed into giving an opinion or taking a stand.
>
> • The domineering person, who makes a habit of "taking over" and imposing his or her own views.
>
> • The person who knows the answer to everything.

know how to respond to something because you simply don't have enough information. If you ask the other for help, in essence, that other person is helping you with your argument. He or she is actually investing in you.

Appeal to a personal sense of ethics – We all have ideas about who we are and what we stand for. And, if we feel that others share those values, it is easier to be more receptive to that person's ideas.

Flattery – Flattery is a two-edged sword that can work either for or against you. Ascribing a good motive to others, even if you don't feel they actually possess one, can make that person easier to work with. Or, in some cases, the other person may actually adjust his thinking to match the motives you have attributed to him. But, if you are insincere, this tactic can backfire.

Be willing to wait for a better deal – A common mistake made by many in the negotiation process is taking the first offer that comes along.

Legitimacy – Legitimacy is another two-edged sword that can be wielded in a manner that depends upon your needs – you can either use it or challenge it. If the other side in the negotiation process has a "legitimate" reason for a decision or a position, find reasons why it is not legitimate.

Use your expertise – If you are considered an expert, you will have a certain amount of influence with those who perceive you to be so. For example, a person with knowledge in a certain area of specialty is more likely to get people to listen to him about changes in that area, especially if the other side is not knowledgeable about the subject.

Divert attention from the major issue – A way of gaining time or easing tensions during the negotiation process is to back off from the main issue for a while. Perhaps there is a secondary issue that can be discussed while you allow the strain over the main issue to ease. Maybe, during these secondary negotiations, a solution to the first problem will be found.

Always request more information – Even if you're sure you understand the position and needs of the other side, request more information. This tactic not only gives you time to consider, but it can make the other side feel that there are some weaknesses in their argument. In the long run, this uncertainty can aid you. The tactic has the additional benefit of drawing the other side out – you might find out something that you were not previously aware of.

Be persistent – A common failure in negotiations is the lack of persistence on the part of the person trying to effect the change. Just because the initial answer is "no," does not mean that the answer will remain negative. The answer may change if asked at a different time, or you might be able to change the mind of the other party by introducing new information or other variables.

Remain positive – A positive attitude is essential to your success in negotiating with others. Even if you fail in obtaining your goals, a good attitude may enable you to achieve them in the future, because you probably will leave the other party with a good impression about you. In addition, maintaining control of yourself throughout the negotiation process will aid you in getting what you want. If you seem relaxed when you should be tense, the other party might feel that you have an extra card up your sleeve. No matter how serious the situation gets, try to control your emotional reaction through the end of the process.

Review – If things seem to bog down after a while, you might try to get things going again by reviewing the positive steps that have been made so far.

Be willing to compromise – Compromise is the soul of negotiation. It would be nice if you could just walk into every meeting and come out with what you want, but it rarely will happen that way. Be willing to make suggestions. In fact, you may want to go into a negotiation meeting with a list of ideas to offer.

The ultimatum – The ultimatum usually is considered to be a "take-it-or-leave-it" proposition. Its success often depends on the time and energy expended by the other side. Sometimes, an ultimatum at the end of an extended process can be effective. First, however, you need to make it palatable to the other side. For an ultimatum to succeed:

•   The other side must have an investment he or she is not prepared to just walk away from.

•   The ultimatum should be made in such a way that it can be reasonably accepted by the other side.

•   You need to back yourself up – show that you have no choice in making the ultimatum.

•   Give the other side several alternatives, making sure that the one you want them to take is the most desirable option available to them.

Negotiating with influence – The amount of influence you have over others, or that they have over you, can play an important role in the negotiating process. Is the person with whom you are negotiating someone who has the power to potentially hurt your career or reputation, either now or in the future? Are you in that position in relationship to the other? While it is rarely good in the long run to come right out and make threats or use this influence, you should be aware of the dynamics involved in such a situation.

Risk-taking – When negotiating, you must be willing to take risks if you want to succeed. The weaker your position, the greater your risk. You need to learn to mix courage with common sense.

Using the known-quantity advantage – If you know the person with whom you will be negotiating, it will be that much easier to make your needs understood (provided, of course, that you are on good terms with the other).

The spirit of fairness – If all else fails, you can throw yourself on the mercy of the other and ask for whatever it is you need out of a sense of fairness and justice. This probably will only work with people who are like you and who share the same sense of justice. Obviously, you wouldn't want to use this method in every situation, but it can be useful at times.

What Things Should You Avoid When Negotiating?

The following are behaviors, attitudes, and other negotiation ploys you should avoid at all costs if you want to be an effective negotiator.

Negotiation Ploys to Avoid

- **Don't be first** – Let the other party in the process give its side of the story first whenever possible. This gives you time to think and adjust your response as necessary.

- **Don't beat around the bush when it is time to express your needs** – If your goals are not clearly stated, how can the other side help you achieve them? Insist on being heard when it is your turn to speak.

- **Don't make assumptions** – Even if the person on the other side of the negotiation table is a friend or, at least, well known, never make assumptions based on this knowledge. Never assume that your needs are understood by this other person either.

- **Don't get emotional** – If you find yourself falling into this trap, remind yourself of the goal or purpose for the negotiation and focus on it to get back on track. To avoid becoming emotionally involved, don't ask questions such as "who is right?" or "what are they trying to do to me?"

- **Don't be arrogant** – If you act as if you are "in charge of the situation" or as if you "know what's best," you are indirectly implying that the other side is inferior. This is a feeling that no one likes to have and, therefore, you increase the likelihood that the other side will want to issue a challenge.

- **Don't intimidate others** – In general, intimidation tactics only make people more resistant to what you have to say or what you are proposing, even if you are entirely reasonable in your requests. If you find that someone is trying to intimidate you, refuse to take the bait and handle it without becoming emotional, if possible.

- **Don't say anything you are not prepared to back up** – If you tell your boss you will get another job if you don't get a raise, you had better mean it. If you say you are willing to live with a compromise, you truly better be able to live with it. If you fail to live up to these expectations, you will lose all credibility in the eyes of the other side.

- **Don't let others control your response** – You should not allow others to be effective when they try to manipulate your reactions. Take time to think the situation through before making a move.

- **Don't let yourself be forced into making rush decisions** – If you find yourself in a negotiation situation unexpectedly, try to stall for time – at least enough to determine what the desired outcome should be. You should do this even if you had no previous position or opinion about the issue. The easiest way to do this is to simply ask for time to think about it.

- **Don't rush things** – If possible, let the other side have time to consider things. Many negotiations fail that could be beneficial to both sides simply because one side was a little too pushy.

- **Don't wait until the last minute** – Whenever possible, make sure there is plenty of time for negotiating. If there are time constraints, it will increase the pressure you feel. If the other side knows about the time constraints, it may be able to take advantage of them.

- **Don't quibble about the result when you've reached it** – Avoid the temptation to go back and revisit certain areas, and don't let others do the same. This lets others know that you are willing to abide by the terms reached, which increases your credibility.

What Should You Do if You Make a Mistake During Negotiations?

Everybody makes mistakes, and, as long as you keep the lines of communication open, they are usually easy to overcome. There are several steps you can take to handle mistakes in the most effective way:

- You must be truly willing to take responsibility for your error and correct it.

- You need to think about the situation without getting so caught up in the possible consequences that you paralyze yourself. Consequences are rarely as bad as we imagine.

- Honestly acknowledge the mistake. If there is a reason for the error, give it. If the other person caused the mistake indirectly due to his or her behavior, express the reason in terms of feelings about the problem rather than emphasizing the other person's faults.

- Reveal the information about the mistake in the way that makes you most comfortable.

- Begin and end the conversation with positive statements, especially if implying some sort of fault in the other person when giving reasons.

What Should You Do if the Negotiation Fails?

You won't always be successful. When the negotiation fails, don't get angry and make rash decisions, and don't just try to ignore the failure and go on as if nothing ever happened. In the first instance, you may irrevocably harm your career or reputation without real cause and, in the second, you may discredit yourself when it comes to future negotiations.

When the process fails, consider doing the following:

- Analyze the situation to discover how it failed. Was it because you weren't properly prepared? Were there legitimate external factors that influenced the outcome?

- Decide how to react. Should you reassess your position and reopen the negotiations? Should new data be introduced? Should you follow through with threats made during an ultimatum?

Whatever you decide to do, no action should be taken until you have given the situation further thought.

Chapter Five Summary

Negotiation is a skill that everyone must undertake. Service providers, particularly those who interact with customers and clients on a regular basis, need to have these skills even more than others. But maintaining quality customer service throughout a negotiation is not an easy thing to do. It is easy to anger people if you misuse negotiation tactics and, even if you make the sale you are working on, you may damage your relationships with others in the future. You and your organization may lose the respect of the public or your clientele for the long term.

While this chapter addresses managing the acceptable, controlled conflict of negotiation, the next chapter addresses the problem of uncontrolled conflict – animosity generated by unhappy customers that can get out of hand and create dangerous situations in the workplace.

Key elements to remember from Chapter Five include:

√   Always treat your customers the way you want to be treated. This will help you maintain a positive environment even in controlled conflicts such as negotiations.

√   You cannot afford to be dishonest in your negotiations – and you don't need to be. You can be persuasive and employ acceptable sales tactics without lowering yourself to using disagreeable sales strategies.

√   Be prepared to back up any claims or promises you make during the course of your negotiations.

√   Find out about the personality type of the person you are negotiating with, and let that help you choose which strategies to use.

√   Accept your mistakes and learn from them.

√   Never, ever take things personally.

√   Remember that you are doing this for your own health, safety, well-being, and future.

CHAPTER SIX

The Difficult Situation: Handling Anger

"One of my problems is that I internalize everything.
I can't express anger; I grow a tumor instead."

– Woody Allen, Comedian

Why Calming Upset People Should Be Important to You

Today, more than ever before in history, providing good service is a survival skill. This is not just because of the need to meet the requirements of employers. It is also to ensure that you have the skills to calm things down when you are interacting with angry, unstable, violent people. Tragically, it is no longer uncommon for angry people to attack customer service personnel and public employees.

Nothing is as important as your health and well-being. And even non-violent confrontations can have some effect on your health in the form of increased stress and stress-related illnesses. For this reason, you need to have anger management skills and learn to apply them so that these confrontations don't have a chance to escalate. In fact, many upset people can be calmed with just a few words and a subtle application of behaviors on your part.

Why Calming Upset People is Important to Your Employer

Aside from protecting employee health and safety, taking care of unhappy customers is an important part of any business's goals. The public has a choice in where it buys its products and services. Ultimately, the public even helps decide which government services are proving valuable and which are not, and those that are seen as unneccesary are likely to see funding cuts. For these reasons, it pays to try to change an unhappy customer's outlook to a positive one.

Your role as a service agent in this endeavor is particularly evident in one statistic from a survey which showed that 68 percent of the customers who don't repeat their business do so because they felt they were treated in a rude manner by one of the organization's employees. Only 14 percent said they didn't return because they weren't happy with the product.

Unfortunately, a customer's unhappiness does not end with his failure to come back. He is likely to tell quite a few other people about the treatment he received, and these people may entirely avoid your company or consider it negatively. An upset customer whose needs are met and who leaves satisfied, on the other hand, is likely to promote a positive image of your organization.

There is another reason to calm down upset customers – they can help your company improve its products and services. It has been found that unhappy customers who take the time to complain are actually more likely to return to the organization than unhappy clients who don't contact the company or agency. Upset members of the public, for this reason, should be viewed as opportunities rather than annoyances. Conflict, therefore, is not something to be avoided, but it is something that must be positively dealt with in a manner that encourages good to come of it. While initially a barrier to the transmission of messages between people, proper control can turn conflict into a revealing communication enhancer.

Is the Problem Really Them?
Or Are We Causing the Trouble?

If a situation gets really out of hand, it is probably your fault. Your job is to keep things under control. Unless a customer is really unstable when he walks in the door, there is almost always something that can be done to de-escalate even the most angry and confrontational situations. Often, it is our own behaviors that create the real problem with a customer. By applying behavioral management strategies, you can help avoid those negative behaviors that are most damaging.

As a service provider, you are going to get angry on occasion. People aren't always reasonable, and you are the person designated to be the target for their frustration. You are going to have bad days, and there are going to be times when somebody pushes all the wrong buttons. This is nothing to feel guilty about. Anger is a natural emotion. But, rather than letting anger rule you, you need to learn to control it and use it to your advantage.

Anger is not always a bad thing. It can give you energy and stamina and, in some situations, it can help you satisfy your needs, because it is hard to conceal and therefore tends to open the floodgates of communication. In some situations, we can take the energy from this anger and use it to take control and be assertive. The presence of anger tells us that something is wrong, and that something must be fixed.

Often, however, it is the negative aspects of anger that we allow to take control. It's not as easy to think straight when we are angry, and this results in bad decisions and impulsive actions that can sometimes be extremely damaging. We also tend to use anger as a weapon when we are embarrassed or hurt, and this only makes things worse. And, if held too long, it can be emotionally and physically draining. Others tend to avoid people who are angry, and, naturally, they form negative images of people who cannot control their emotions. And, of course, anger breeds rapidly. It can escalate to the point of violence.

Looking at Ourselves: What Makes Us Tick? What Makes Us Explode?

What makes you angry? We all have different boiling points, but there are certain things we all do to ourselves that impact our emotions. We often actually "think" ourselves into angered states. The following is a list of some of our self-destructive behaviors:

- **Thinking Ahead** – How many times have you planned out a confrontation that never materialized when you actually met the person you expected would make you angry? By assuming that a situation can only be resolved by confrontation, we set the stage for it.

- **Name-Calling** – When we get angry with others, we often call them names, if only in our own minds. For example: "He's a jerk." The problem with this is that it promotes unwarranted negative feelings toward that person. He may have done something you are justified in being angry about, but he

Do You Need to Get Your Anger Under Control?

If you find that anger is creating any of the following, you may have a potentially dangerous problem with anger:

- It makes you aggressive
- It causes problems in your relationships with others
- It lasts a long time – too long
- It happens frequently
- It's too intense

probably has many good characteristics that you may forget exist behind the negative label of "jerk."

- **Inventing** – We often invent causes of anger when we assume we know what another person is thinking. These assumptions are frequently wrong, because everybody looks at things in a different way. We allow ourselves to be angry about things that we have imagined.

- **We Exaggerate** – Frequently, we blow things way out of proportion and allow our emotions to run rampant. Because we are not thinking clearly, we lose sight of the fact that the cause of our anger is really pretty insignificant.

- **We Judge People Unfairly** – We frequently

decide how people should act or should have acted in a specific situation. This is unfair, because we are really inventing circumstances in which we should have gotten our own way. It fails to take into account that there may be very good reasons for the way another person reacted.

Does Every Conflict Need a Winner and a Loser?

Sometimes in today's world it seems that every conflict has to have a winner and a loser, but the best service providers recognize that this simply isn't true. They are the ones who work for the win-win situation. There are five basic ways to resolve conflicts:

1. **A Dropped Ball** – Avoiding the problem or failing to resolve it is a lose-lose occurrence in which no one wins because the problem never gets truly aired. The customer goes away unhappy and unable to get help, and he probably won't come back.

2. **Winner Takes All** – ("You bought it. It's your problem now.") In this scenario, supposedly a win-lose situation, one side gets everything his way and the other gets nothing. In public service terms, this usually means that the customer is the loser, and this is self-defeating in the long run because that customer and anyone he talks to about your organization will likely never be back. This is really a hidden lose-lose situation.

3. **Compromise** – ("I'll give you this if you'll give me that.") This approach is frequently used in service, and it certainly has its place,

although there is some risk regarding customer satisfaction. Neither side wins, but neither side loses.

4.   **Accommodation** – ("The warranty has expired, but we'll take care of it anyway.") In this case, the customer is the obvious winner, but in the long run, the company may also be the winner. At times, it is better to take a smaller initial loss (such as the price of a repair) than a greater loss (such as an account with a major buyer). This often is a hidden win-win philosophy.

5.   **Working Together** – ("We can fix this.") This is the one to strive for – the win-win method in which everyone leaves the interaction happy and satisfied. It often requires creative thinking, and it certainly calls for a positive approach and a willingness on both sides to understand the other person's point of view.

What Does the Public Want From You?

It doesn't matter whether a customer is calm or upset, there are certain things he wants or expects when he makes a complaint to someone in your organization:

- The customer wants to be listened to. Sometimes, in fact, this is all a customer needs. He needs to get his feelings off his chest, and he needs to feel that it has done some good.

- The customer wants to be treated with

respect. He has paid for a service or product either out-of-pocket or through his taxes, and he therefore feels he has the right to be treated well. He is right.

- He wants the problem fixed quickly, and, if possible, he wants some sort of compensation that rewards him for the trouble he has had. This compensation can be as simple as an apology, or it can be in the form of an upgraded replacement or a discount on future services.

- If the customer is angry due to the way he has been treated or because he was promised something that was not deliverable, he wants that service provider to be punished in some way or otherwise suffer consequences for his actions.

- He wants easy access to service, and he expects that service to be of good quality.

- He doesn't want to lose. There doesn't have to be a winner and a loser, and a win-win ending will make everybody happy.

- In some cases, the customer may simply desire assurances that such a problem will never occur again.

What Do Service Providers Do That Makes the Public Angry?

Customers become upset for a number of reasons, many of which don't have much to do with the product or service an organization provides. These include:

- **Unmet Expectations** – This could be related to how a customer expected to be treated or how he thought a product would work or what a service would provide.

- **A Powerless Feeling** – A customer who feels powerless may be frustrated and angry about the problem.

- **Untrained Personnel** – People rarely want to be the test subject for a trainee. They want their problems to be handled by people who know what to do.

- **Dislike the Organization** – People who have had previous bad experiences with the company or have heard negative things about the company may react more angrily when something goes wrong than they would otherwise.

- **It's the Only Way** – Some people think the only way they will get their needs met is to be angry and demand service.

- **Discourtesy** – Naturally, people are angry when they feel they have been treated without respect.

- **Ignored** – People who feel they are being ignored or put off, such as those whose phone calls are not returned, react angrily.

- **Conflicting Stories** – When people are told one thing by one employee, and something else by another, they naturally become angry, because it appears that someone is lying to them.

- **Argument** – If someone in the company has argued with the customer, the customer will often have to be handled carefully in order to return him to a state of calmness.

- **Feelings Invalidated** – When people are told that they shouldn't feel a certain way, it often angers them, because it implies that their feelings are unimportant or wrong.

- **Previous State** – If a customer is already upset, tired, or under stress when he comes in, it is easy for him to be set off.

- **Frustration** – If the person is having difficulty getting help, he can easily become angry. For example, a person who is transferred from department to department may lose his temper, particularly if he feels helpless.

- **Honesty is Challenged** – A person who feels that his integrity is being questioned will often react with anger.

- **Embarrassment** – People are angry when they are embarrassed, and they often lash out unfairly.

- **Vindication** – Some customers are determined to prove themselves right, whether it is really necessary or not.

- **Failure to Listen** – Those who feel as if they are not given a chance to tell their side of the story often react extremely negatively.

- **Personality** – Some people are just naturally contrary, and they don't need much of an excuse to fly off the handle.

- **Personal Prejudices** – Everybody has prejudices, and some people are unable to control them. The customer may be prejudiced against your skin color, your company, your cologne, your hair color, or virtually anything else conceivable.

- **Manipulation** – Some people use anger as a method of intentionally manipulating others.

What Can You Do to Reduce Anger in Others?

The following tips can help you reduce or prevent anger in those you are providing services for:

Things To Do To Reduce Anger

- Think before you act or say anything.

- Always act in a professional manner.

- Your body posture should be open, confident, and non-threatening. Don't cross your arms or lean on your hands if you are sitting at a desk or standing at a tall counter.

- Allow the other person to set a non-threatening interaction distance.

- Use the other person's name at the beginning of a sentence when things seem out of control. People listen better when they hear their names.

- Breathe slowly to help yourself think rationally.

- Cultivate a calm, interested voice. Don't let emotions such as annoyance or irritation come through in your vocal tones.

- Have a glass of water on hand. When you are under stress, your voice may become hoarse. Drink something to alleviate this so that you can maintain pleasant vocal tones.

- Use a confident, but non-condescending tone of voice.

- Be calm and soothing, but not irritatingly so.

- Recognize how you, as an individual, respond to stress so that you can modify your behavior when the danger signs first appear.

- Always listen carefully to what the other has to say, and try to determine what is not being said.

- Return to your point. Don't let yourself get diverted by another's behavior or language.

- Use words that don't imply blame or make others react defensively.

- Take notes so that you don't have to ask the customer to repeat himself.

- If you are not sure that you understand

something, ask questions so you don't further anger the customer by wasting time on a
problem that doesn't exist.

- Always be sure that the customer understands the instructions you are giving in an
effort to resolve the customer's problem.

- Know your limitations. If you know that you
do not do well under certain circumstances,
get help from someone who can give the
customer the proper respect.

- If a customer is yelling, try requesting that
he speak "more slowly" instead of asking
him to "stop yelling." When he slows down,
his volume will probably decrease at the
same time.

- If necessary, take a break so you can get control of yourself again.

- Give positive forms of feedback so the customer knows whether you are properly
understanding the messages he intends to
send.

- Treat the customer with respect, no matter
what the circumstances, and no matter how
badly he is behaving.

- Say "please" and "thank you." Be polite and
don't let stress take your fundamental man-
ners away from you.

- Take care of the problem as thoroughly and
quickly as possible so that it doesn't come
up again.

- Be organized. Present yourself in a manner that shows that you know what you are doing and that you are in control of the situation and are on top of your job. (Note: You control yourself and your job, never the customer.)

- Return all phone calls from the public promptly.

Things To Avoid To Help Reduce Anger

- Never, ever take things personally.

- Avoid any unpleasant facial expressions. Don't let negative emotions cross your face in the form of a scowl or rolling your eyes. Even if you don't think the customer can see you, there's a chance that he will. Also, other customers may note the expression and assume you feel the same way when you interact with them.

- Don't move sluggishly when responding to the person's needs. You don't need to rush, but move in a manner that shows that you understand that the customer's time is valuable.

- Don't smoke, chew gum, or eat in front of the customer or while you are on the phone. Avoid any other behaviors that could be construed as rude.

- Don't talk to your computer screen. Never allow your computer or any other office objects to become a barrier to communication. It is the customer you are interacting with, not the furniture.

- Don't sigh. This implies that you are impatient, annoyed, or tired of listening to the customer.

- Never use vulgar language or insult the customer.

- Don't speak over the customer when he is talking.

- Don't interrupt the customer, even if you think you know what he has to say.

- Never touch an upset person. This can trigger a violent episode.

- Don't give orders or make demands when speaking to the customer.

- Avoid anything which implies a criticism of the customer.

- Don't allow yourself to be distracted by anything else while interacting with the customer. He deserves your complete, undivided attention.

- Never allow your personal prejudices to prevent you from treating a customer with the proper respect.

- Don't avoid complainants. If an angry customer wants to talk to you, handle it immediately, and don't pass the responsibility off to someone else. Things will only be worse if you wait. If you are personally requested and you don't feel you should be alone with the customer, or you don't feel you can separate your emotions from the interaction, have your supervisor or someone else present who can help you keep things calm.

How to Keep a Handle
On Your Own Emotions

There are things you can do to prevent yourself from overreacting to difficult customers while still managing the interaction effectively. They include:

- If things get overly intense, take a break from the situation, even if it is only for a few seconds. Excuse yourself in a polite manner, and be sure to give the customer a legitimate reason for leaving.

- If a customer is making unreasonable demands, try rephrasing and repeating yourself. For instance, if a customer insists on immediate repairs when the repairman will not be in until the next day, you might use these statements: "The repairman won't be in until tomorrow." "I'm sorry, but he's already gone for the day." "I'll see to it that he gets to it first thing in the morning." Eventually, if you remain calm, the message is likely to get through, particularly if your behaviors show your sincerity.

- If you have tried to solve the problem and can't seem to satisfy the customer, ask him what you can do to make him happy. Sometimes, they want less than you would expect.

- Be alert for potential violence. Look for the following nonverbal cues that potentially violent people often display:

  - Clenched fists
  - Enraged facial expressions
  - Flared nostrils
  - A tense body
  - Flushed skin tones
  - Leaning forward
  - Shouting
  - Angry, tense vocal tones

- If threatened, call for assistance immediately. Don't take any risks.

- Recognize the things that make you defensive. Assert yourself when it is productive to do so and avoid doing so if it is not.

- Learn to laugh at yourself.

- Learn to trust others and forgive them.

- Understand that anger is a personal choice. You don't have to succumb to it.

- Know your body. If sugar makes you antsy, avoid it. If drinking makes you angry, don't drink. Do things for yourself that are physically and emotionally positive.

- Don't rationalize your anger. Take responsibility for your emotions.

- Don't try to reason with a person who seems

to be drunk or on drugs (and don't accuse anyone of drinking or taking drugs). Call for assistance, if necessary.

- Don't keep thinking about the things that made you angry. Don't replay or repeat the scene over and over in your mind.

- Cultivate a friend you can talk things over with and who will set you straight if you seem to become overly intense about minor things.

- Learn to overlook the petty things that don't really matter. Don't allow yourself to fret about the irrelevant.

- Maintain a positive self-esteem. Don't beat yourself up over things.

- Don't live in denial. Recognize the varied forms of anger that we disguise from our-selves – these include annoyance, irritation, and frustration.

- Learn to treat others as equals, and give them the benefit of the doubt. Try to under-stand how they feel about the situation.

- Don't try to control others.

Chapter Six Summary

In this chapter, you learned a lot of information about what makes people angry and how to prevent confrontations from getting worse. When considering how to apply all this information, it may seem to be a bit overwhelming. In fact, however, you'll find that it is fairly simple to apply these behaviors and techniques. The most important thing to remember is to treat the customer with the utmost respect.

Key elements to remember from Chapter Six include:

√   You need to learn to manage confrontations, because today's environment can be a dangerous one. To ensure your safety, you must know how to head things off before violence can occur. Anger management is a survival skill.

√   Anger is a natural emotion. You won't be able to stop it from happening. But you need to learn to control it rather that letting it control you.

√   It is easy for people to "think" themselves into confrontation. Recognize this tendency in yourself and in those with whom you interact.

√   Know what the causes of customer anger are, and learn to produce an cnvironment that discourages it.

√   Never, ever take things personally.

√   Remember that you are doing this for your own health, safety, well-being, and future.

CHAPTER SEVEN

Managing Stress and Burnout

*"Troubles are only mental; it is the mind that manufactures them,
and the mind can gorge them, banish
them, abolish them."*

Mark Twain

What Do Stress and Burnout Have to Do With Customer Service?

When service providers burn out or experience undue stress, they are irritable, quick to anger, and likely to over-react to the slightest provocation. When you are working with the public, you can't afford to let these behaviors impact the rapport you need to establish with your customers. You cannot afford to tarnish your career or your organization's reputation.

Employee burnout, which is the eventual byproduct of repeated and enduring stress, can cause service providers to react in numerous ways that negatively impact their job performance. Customer service jobs are not easy – they require you to accept and manage behaviors from others that you might not be willing to accept in any other circumstance. You have to be polite when others are rude, nice when others are irritable, and helpful when others are intractable. This can be extremely wearing over time, causing an elevated level of stress and eventual burnout.

And not every employer is knowledgeable or tolerant of the effects of this long-term stress. It is not unusual to hear of people being fired or reprimanded for the inappropriate actions of employees who eventually and predictably react to this stress. In just a moment's thoughtless, emotional reaction, you could lose everything you have worked for.

Why We All Need a 30,000 Mile Tune-Up

Nobody ever said that being a service provider is an easy task. When you have to deal with emotionally charged situations on a frequent basis, it can be exhausting. Under such circumstances, it is easy to succumb to burnout, and those who are suffering from burnout have less energy, and therefore don't have the emotional reserve needed for demanding circumstances. This can only lead to poor performance.

It doesn't have to be that way, however. By giving yourself a 30,000 mile tune-up when you recognize the early warning signs of

burnout, you can avoid the problem altogether.
These signals include:

- **Your Temper** – If you find that things are setting you off that never bothered you before, consider it a warning This sign can be as subtle as increased irritation over changing traffic lights or the sounds of somebody chewing gum.

- **Complaints** – If you find yourself continuously complaining about things or repeating your complaints to others, you may have a problem.

- **Cynicism** – If you become irritated at the positive emotions displayed by others, or are cynical of how happy others appear to be, you may be approaching burnout.

- **Absentmindedness** – If you begin losing your ability to concentrate, you may be displaying burnout symptoms. This could be illustrated by things such as forgetting what you are doing.

- **Interruptions** – People closing in on burnout frequently enjoy interruptions as a distraction.

- **Stress** – If you find that you are displaying stress symptoms more and more frequently, it's time to take a step away.

- **Dependency** – Do you need caffeine to get you through the day? Are you drinking more or taking relaxation pills? These are strong warning signals.

- **Inertia or Apathy** – If you have less energy than you used to or just feel that you don't want to do anything when you get home from work, you probably need a break to prevent burnout.

- **Tardiness** – People who are suffering from burnout are frequently late in getting to work or returning from breaks.

- **Feeling Less Communicative** – If your behaviors change, and you don't like to interact with others as much as you used to, it may be an indicator of burnout.

The most notable symptom may be chronic tension. Tension is often caused by people who suppress their natural emotions. As a service provider, you may have to do this on a regular basis if you are continually confronted by angry, irritated people. Muscular tension is similar to armor. It builds up over time as we barricade our emotions. It has several negative effects:

- It inhibits relaxation
- It causes pain
- It interferes with physical sensations
- It reduces the circulation of blood
- It restricts movement
- It inhibits the ability to breathe deeply
- It prevents emotional expression
- It takes energy needed for more positive activities

Dealing With Burnout Once You Realize It's Knocking On the Door

Burnout does not have to be a fact of life for service personnel. There are some concrete things you can do to prevent it or head it off before it gets out of control. Many of these are also short-term solutions to stress. These include:

- **Set Goals** – Rather than just plodding through each day or each task as it comes, set goals for yourself and start working to achieve them. If you have a major goal, break it down on paper into smaller, easily manageable steps you need to complete in order to achieve that goal. That way, you'll feel good as you progress down the list. Minor but important job-oriented goals also work in improving your outlook, because you'll feel a sense of accomplishment as you reach them.

- **Don't Be Shy** – If you've been doing a good job and no one seems to notice and you start feeling put upon because of it, speak up. Point out the good things you have been doing. Don't be afraid to show you think positively about the work you have been doing.

- **Physical Exercise** – Exercise stimulates blood flow to the brain and energizes you, giving you the fuel you need to get through the day.

- **Take Care of Yourself** – Do the things that are right for you. Speak up when you feel you are being ignored.

- **Don't Allow Yourself to Simmer** – If a co-worker, employer, or family member is doing something that upsets you, get it off your chest by talking privately to that person in a friendly, tactful way.

- **Pay Attention to the Needs of Others** – Try doing good deeds for your co-workers. Be helpful to friends and family members, even if it takes some extra effort on your part.

- **Avoid Resentment** – Instead of resenting people if they get things you want or seem to lack consideration for your needs, take care of yourself. Be direct in asking for the things you want and, if you don't get them, figure out ways you can work to achieve your goals.

- **Avoid Gossiping About Negative Things** – This only creates negative energy and bad attitudes. It also makes people feel guilty, and you don't need that.

- **Reward Yourself** – Find out what makes you feel good and use it. If taking a breather and flipping through a magazine on your break helps you relax more than drinking coffee with co-workers, then find a private place to enjoy the magazine. If taking your child's picture out for a quick peek is effective, use that. Use pens that you like to hold and note paper that you like to look at; wear a favorite piece of jewelry.

The best way to avoid burnout is to not let it happen. You don't have to let yourself succumb to negative energy. When you feel it approaching, do something to head it off.

Since burnout is really the result of long-term stress, it can be prevented by managing stress before it can build up to dangerous proportions. Throughout every day of your life, you encounter numerous stressful events. Normally, you can just deal with the problems that cause the stress reaction, and then go on. But, sometimes, it is not so easy to handle the stress. A person who cares for a child with a serious illness, for example, cannot cure his own stress simply because he gives the child an aspirin. The caregiver must learn to cope with stress.

What are the
Causes of Stress?

Anytime you need to adjust to some sort of change, you experience stress. Not every form of stress is negative – it can even be an exhilarating sensation. When you participate in or observe sporting events, for example, you are experiencing positive stress. In fact, the closer the competing scores become, the greater the stress is, and the more you enjoy the game.

There are three sources for stress:

- The Mind
- The Body
- The Environment

Just as people can "think" themselves into anger, they can also "think" themselves into having stress reactions. When you worry about what others think of you, or when you worry about the future or the consequences of some action, your thinking is engendering stress. Lack of exercise, illness, and poor diet can also cause stress. Your body is conditioned with a "fight or flight" instinct. Your responses to dangerous situations can cause stress, which you must learn to relieve. Interestingly, however, we all interpret "danger" differently. An offer of friendship may even evoke this instinctive response to some, while others would never even consider a relationship to be potentially dangerous.

Environmental factors which can cause stress are also numerous – time, the people around you, noise, pollution, the weather, social demands, and so on. To the customer service provider, this external form of stress is probably the most debilitating, especially if it continues over a long period of time.

How Can You Tell if You Are Suffering From Stress?

Stress can manifest itself both physically and mentally. Usually, however, it is first signaled by muscular tension. Neck aches, muscle aches, backaches, stomachaches – all these can be caused by the tension of stress. Stress can also have negative effects on your digestion and your energy level. Mentally, stress can show itself through irritability, explosive emotions, hysteria, irrational thinking, and so on.

One method you can use for identifying your stress-related symptoms is to close your eyes and consciously think about your physical and mental states. Are you tense? Can you easily force your-

COMMON SYMPTOMS OF STRESS

Addiction	Hostility
Anger	Inability to Relax
Anxiety	Indigestion
Backache	Insomnia
Body Tension	Irrational Thinking
Bowel Irritation	Irritability
Concentration Problems	Muscular Tics/Spasms
Constipation	Neck Ache
Dependency	Obsession
Depression	Physical Weakness
Diarrhea	Powerless Feeling
Emotional Explosiveness	Resentment
Exhaustion	Self-Esteem Issues
Fears/Phobias	Sleep Disorders
Gas	Stomachache
Headache	Trembling
High Blood Pressure	Ulcers
Hopeless Feeling	Weight Problems

self to relax? Have you been saying things that you quickly regret? Do things seem to get overwhelming at times? Becoming aware of yourself in this way can help you ease the stress as well as put things in perspective. Both physical and mental stress signals, however, could be indicative of other problems such as illness or disease. These symptoms should not be ignored.

What Can You Do to Reduce Your Stress Level?

Everybody experiences stress in a unique way, and what may reduce stress in one person may not help you. However, there are numerous ways to counteract the problem. Some find exercise to be the strongest cure, while others choose deep breathing exercises and meditation. There are methods that, with long-term and repeated usage, can reduce your overall level of stress permanently, while other strategies can help you quickly relieve the tensions of the moment.

Among the stress-reduction strategies you can use are:

- **Relaxation Techniques** – Stress and relaxation cannot exist within you at the same time, so learning how to quickly and consciously relax your muscles can help you to quickly relieve the symptoms of stress. Deep breathing exercises have the same effect. There are techniques that can teach your body to quickly respond to verbal instructions to relax.

- **Meditation** – You can reduce your stress level by taking time for yourself. Meditation is an activity in which you shut out the external demands of life and turn your thoughts inward. By setting aside your daily worries and concerns for a few moments each day, you can reduce stress and simultaneously promote clearer thinking.

- **Positive Thinking** – Negative thoughts can increase your level of stress. Many times, we play out negative scenarios of what we think will happen only to have things turn out much better than we expect. We waste energy and stress on events that never take place. By focusing on the positive, you can prevent stress while simultaneously improving your outlook. Imagine positive scenarios instead of negative ones.

- **Thought-Stopping Techniques** – If you are one of the many people who let their mind race in circles about their problems, inducing unnecessary stress, you may want to learn methods for quickly stopping these thoughts so you can relax. These types of obsessions range from self-doubts to phobias. Thought-stopping, combined with positive thinking afterward, can prevent fears and negative emotions from getting out of control.

- **Self-Hypnosis** – There are several self-hypnosis and subliminal techniques that can help you relax and relieve the symptoms of stress. People who experience severe injury or shock can self-induce themselves into therapeutic trances to minimize physical trauma on the body. There are books that can tell you of these techniques, and there are audio tapes of relaxing music which contain positive subliminal suggestions for relieving stress.

- **Healthy Nutrition** – A poor diet can cause

or add to stress. If you don't get the proper balance of nutrients, you may develop a type of malnutrition that goes unnoticed, because it lacks readily recognizable and obvious symptoms. A poor reaction to stress is, however, often one of the results. There are numerous books available regarding diet and stress. The B vitamins and calcium are helpful in coping with stress.

• **Take Charge of Your Life** – As a service provider, you have to interact with people regularly. The way in which you do this strongly impacts your level of stress. People who are assertive and positive will suffer fewer stress-related problems than will those who are walked on or bullied. Everybody is assertive some of the time and in specific types of circumstances – you need to cultivate a positive self-esteem and be willing to stand up for yourself at the appropriate times.

The above lists only a few of the many strategies for reducing long-term stress problems. Several other methods are discussed more fully in the next few sections of this chapter.

Using Exercise to Exorcise Stress Reactions

In the modern world, exercise does not come naturally. We all have busy schedules and most of us believe we just don't have time to exercise regularly. Yet exercise is probably the simplest, most effective way to relieve the tensions we experience on a daily basis. We know that exercise is good for our bodies, but not everybody is aware of the benefits it has for the state of our minds.

The exercise you get while going about your normal daily

routine is probably not enough. According to one report, only one in four people actually gets enough exercise. You do not have to go to a gym or fitness center to benefit from the value of stress-reducing physical activity. Even a few minutes of stretching on a daily basis can help you function better.

There are two basic types of exercise. Aerobic exercises are those which require a lot of oxygen and involve large muscle groups. They increase your heart rate. These exercises include running, brisk walking, and dancing.

To built up stamina and strengthen your cardiovascular system, you would need to perform this type of exercise three to four times a week for approximately 20 minutes at a time. Before beginning this type of program, it is recommended that you talk to your doctor, because overdoing it can put a strain on your heart and cause other physical difficulties.

The second type of exercise is far less intense. This includes stretching and toning activities that increase your flexibility and muscle strength. For those who are out of shape and unable to perform aerobic activity, this type of exercise can be used to build up stamina so that you can exercise more intensely. Walking slowly, doing housework, and performing other daily activities are examples of this form of low-intensity exercise.

Clock-Watching – Stress in the Busy, Modern World

Are you always on the go? Are you always rushing to get somewhere? Do you never seem to get places on time or do you continuously miss deadlines? Do you have a hard time making decisions when none of your alternatives are ideal? Do you feel overwhelmed? Does it seem like you spend all your time doing things you don't want to do? Are you always tired? Do you spend hours that you should be doing something else just sort of listlessly doing nothing? Do you never have time for personal relationships?

If this sounds like you, you may have a time-management problem – one of the most stressful byproducts of our modern society. Many of us just move from activity to activity without any real thought. We get things done when we have to, but we often delay or complete these projects with less efficiency than we could have. We procrastinate and we wait for a deadline to come before we complete tasks that could have been done without the added stress in a more timely manner.

To overcome the strain of time-management problems, you must force yourself to become a strategic planner. This entails three activities:

- Making Decisions
- Setting Priorities
- Scheduling

To get started with this type of project, try keeping track of how you spend your time during the day. Write down the things you do and note when and how long they take. Then, look back and decide how you should have done things differently. Begin your planning based on what you see. You probably won't fix all your time problems right away, but you may be able to eliminate some of your biggest worries. There are many resources that can help you overcome this problem.

What to Do When Nothing You Do Works at Relieving Stress

If you are suffering from chronic stress, you probably will not be able to overcome your problems overnight. It's not easy to make changes to your lifelong habits. Even if you do feel success at first, you may find yourself reverting back to those old, unhealthy habits.

This is part of the normal process of change. If you find yourself making excuses about why you are not doing some of the stress relieving activities you promised yourself you would do, you might find it helpful to have a little talk with yourself – remind yourself of your reasons for trying to reduce your stress level in the first place. Remind yourself of the consequences you were facing from being overly stressed.

As a service provider, the consequences of stress reactions in your workplace can be severe. You could cause someone else to be harmed, you could lose your job, you could escalate a dangerous situation with an unstable customer. . . . You don't need any of that – and you don't deserve it. Controlling your stress level is about controlling your life.

Chapter Seven Summary

Employee burnout and stress are major concerns in any organization. Unfortunately, not all employers are aware of this. As a result, it is your responsibility as a service provider and as a human being who wants a safe, happy, and productive life to manage your stress level and increase your physical and mental health.

Your job as a service provider is already difficult – the people you have to interact with are not always reasonable. You don't want to add to your professional problems by ignoring the consequences of stress.

Key elements to remember from Chapter Seven include:

√   Recognize the danger of burnout that exists for every customer service provider.

√   There are short-term solutions to stress that you can begin to use immediately, or you can begin regular long-term programs that will improve your quality of life and enhance your reactions to stress.

√   Because there are so many ways in which you can relieve the symptoms of stress and even eliminate their causes, you can choose a method which suits you best.

√   Physical exercise, even if it is just an increase in how active you are on a daily basis, is one of the simplest and most beneficial forms overall for stress reduction.

√   Never, ever take things personally.

√   Remember that you are doing this for your own health, safety, well-being, and future.

CHAPTER EIGHT

Damage Control

"A want of tact is worse than a want of virtue."

Benjamin Disraeli, English Prime Minister

So We Made a Mistake . . . What's the Big Deal?
How Can You Repair Your Personal Reputation?
Practicing the Fine Art of the Sincere Apology and Accountability
How Can You Protect Your Organization's Reputation?
Can Behavior Management be Applied to Organizations?
We Didn't Just Make a Little Mistake – We Blew It!
What Kind of Things Can Be Done to Enhance an Image?

So We Made a Mistake . . .
What's the Big Deal?

You or someone within your organization made a small mistake. It may not be a big deal to you, but it probably is to the customer who lost time, money, or both because of it. If you don't do something to make up for the mistake, you may lose that customer forever. Furthermore, that unhappy person may prejudice others against you or your company.

The degree of mistake does not always dictate the severity of action you must take to correct it. Often, correcting the mistake and apologizing sincerely will be enough. At other times, more stringent actions will be necessary. The worst thing you can do when you make a mistake, however, is nothing.

When you are responsible for a wrongdoing – even a minor, unintentional one – you can lose the trust of your customers and the public in general. When people buy a product, they expect it to work. They will be frustrated or even angry if it doesn't work, but they generally understand that errors do happen. They trust you to fix the problem. They will only lose trust in your organization if you fail to meet that expectation.

How Can You Repair
Your Personal Reputation?

Unless you own your own business, you have to answer to employers as well as customers. That's why your personal reputation as a service provider or company representative is so important. If you make a mistake, you need to repair the problem and avoid damaging your reputation.

Mistakes are not all bad. Without making mistakes, we don't learn. You can protect yourself from the damages of these problems with a variety of behavior management techniques. You need to do one of the following:

- Reduce the negative impression
- Negate the negative impression

- Neutralize the negative impression
- Redefine the negative impression as positive

Practicing the Fine Art of the Sincere Apology and Accountability

How you make an apology can also impact your success in repairing a relationship with a customer. When you give an apology, you admit to responsibility for the act and try to obtain forgiveness from the injured party or observer. Apologies serve the following functions.

- They show that you recognize the offending behavior as wrong.

- They show that you are willing to take responsibility for your actions.

- They show that you want to repair the damage.

Frequently in customer service situations, the apology is not enough. You must also explain what happened. The most common way to atone for a mistake is by giving an account of what happened. There are two types of accounts: Excuses and justifications.

When you give an excuse, you explain an event but try to reduce your personal responsibility. For example, you might make a statement such as this:

"Thank you for bringing this to my attention. I thought I was giving you the right instructions. I only learned how to use this program yesterday, and I must have hit the wrong key."

In this example, the customer service agent explains what happens, but places the blame on improper training or inexperience.

In such a situation, he can further assure the customer or client that the new information being given is accurate by adding the following statement:

> "This time, I had my supervisor check the data to make sure I'm giving you the right information. It won't happen again."

The second form of account is the justification – this is an explanation that attempts to make a wrongful act appear positive. In this situation, you admit that you are responsible, but you try to show the action in a positive light. You attempt to turn a negative event into a positive one. For instance, you might give the following statement to a customer.

> "I e-mailed you the wrong instructions, but it actually turns out better this way. We updated the instructions just this morning, so you will be getting the latest information. I'll get the right ones out to you immediately."

The success of the accounts you give on a personal basis will be highly dependent on how others already perceive you. For example, an employee who is always on time will be believable when he gives an excuse for tardiness. A person who is chronically late, however, will have a more difficult time convincing anyone of his innocence.

The following guidelines will help you when you need to justify or excuse your actions.

- Excuses should not be overused, or they will be less credible.

- Be cautious in how you use justifications. A customer who thinks something is a "big deal" will only be angered by any attempts you make to minimize the importance of the occurrence.

•   Always be sincere. If the customer feels that
         your explanations are insincere, you will
         lose credibility, and the customer might feel
         as if he or she is being manipulated. This
         will instantly destroy any rapport you have
         established with the customer.

•   Remember those who are harmed – if your
         actions are likely to injure a person or group
         of people, you must express sincere concern
         for this occurrence.

How Can You Protect Your Organization's Reputation?

You cannot single-handedly protect your organization's reputation. It must have strong, effective policies that all people within conscientiously abide by. If you make a mistake and apologize for it, the customer may very well accept your apology, but still blame the organization. This happens when a company has a bad image in the public mind, or when the customer has heard bad things from other people about the company.

If a company is perceived as one which cares about the people who buy its products and services, then customers will be more likely to shrug off a negative encounter with a service representative – particularly if that service provider attempted to make amends when the mistake was discovered.

Excuses, justifications, and apologies work the same way on an organizational level as they do regarding an individual. If your company offers reasonable accounts for its actions, it is less likely to suffer damages than it would if it were to remain silent or overuse its excuses. Consider the problem one community newspaper faced after its competitor folded.

The newspaper, which relies on the legal advertisements from the county and surrounding municipalities as its major source of income, immediately raised its prices upon the demise of the competing newspaper. The governmental entities in the surrounding communities were shocked at the dramatic increase in rates, because their budgeting had been based on the old rates. When asked for a justification for the new rates, the newspaper's managing editor merely pointed out that the new rates were still well under the maximum allowable under the law. When the other newspaper reopened under new management a short time later and became eligible to carry the government legal notices, the angry officials chose to advertise in the new publication.

The newspaper's managing editor was perfectly within his rights to raise the rates, but his explanation was not adequate. If he had truthfully explained that he had been charging less than cost during the price wars with the other newspaper that eventually folded, the government officials would likely have been more understanding and may not have been so quick to switch publications when the opportunity arose.

An organization or company is much like a person when it comes to how people perceive it. Its reputation depends on what people think of it. But, while your reputation depends on the thoughts and goodwill of perhaps a few dozen people, the organization's depends on that of thousands, hundreds of thousands, or even millions. While you may have little or no trouble maintaining the good will of a few dozen people, it is almost an impossible task for an organization to satisfy everyone.

This task is further complicated by the differece between how people view organizations and how they view individual people. While no one expects you to be perfect, organizations, agencies, and companies are often held to a higher standard. Because of this, everything that impacts the company's image takes on particular importance.

When people come to a company or organization, they come with expectations. When a company has a good reputation, people have high expectations. When it has a bad reputation, the public's expectations are lower.

If a company with a good reputation fails to live up to the customer's expectations, there is a good chance that the customer will discount the negative encounter. If the company has a bad reputation, however, there is a good chance that the customer will not be back – ever.

Can Behavior Management be Applied to Organizations?

As a public service provider, you should understand that every aspect of your job – and everyone else's within your organization – can either add to or detract from the company's reputation. This means that behavior management strategies can be applied to organizations.

Your personal behaviors are important to your organization. For instance, the way employees dress and act when interacting with the public will reflect on the organization. The image the organization tries to create through its employees should be appropriate for the company's most important target audience. A formal demeanor can hurt some organizations, while an informal style would damage others. The organization's behavior as a collective entity is also critical to its success.

Your company's methods of dealing with the public and its concerns are an important part of how the organization is perceived by the public, but it is only one part of the equation. The company's involvement with the community, the way in which it treats its employees, and the way in which it deals with crises and accidents are just a few of the other factors the public will use in deciding how it feels about the organization.

An organization that provides good service can still get a tarnished reputation, for example, if it is always in the news because its employees are continuously filing lawsuits or going on strike for better working conditions. The way in which a beleaguered company handles a layoff situation can also make a difference in how it is perceived by the community. Whether your organization is public or private, word will get out about how it conducts business, and this will eventually trickle down to impact your success in providing customer service.

In a small industry or in a company located in a moderate-sized community, your individual reputation and actions will have a greater impact on how your company is perceived as a whole. In these smaller environments, it is easier for a person to be strongly associated with an organization. In some cases, people "are" the organizations they represent – at least in the mind of the public.

We Didn't Just Make a Little Mistake – We Blew It!

Image management is never more important to an organization than during a crisis. The behavior of all people within the company takes on added importance during these times and during the following months when the public's memory of the crisis is still clear.

Frequently, the cause of a mistake – even a large one – is less important to the public than how an organization responds to it. For example, a major oil company suffered a severe blow to its reputation after an oil spill in the late 1980s. The company reacted by understating the impacts of the disaster, by giving conflicting statements, by not taking full and immediate responsibility for the incident, and by constantly changing strategies while trying to manage the emergency.

There are seven steps that can help a company get through a time of great crisis.

- Respond quickly. While you do need to take time to assess the situation, immediate reaction is necessary.

- Organize your response rather than react to individual events.

- Inform the public and those with a need to know and keep them informed as new information becomes available.

- Take the proper actions called for by the event.

- Take responsibility for the wrongdoing rather than trying to refocus blame or reduce liability.

- Remember the victim by acting in a responsive, compassionate manner.

- Re-establish public confidence in your product or services.

Researchers Dr. Donald Slowik and Cara Cantarella, in a book entitled, *The Power of Impression Management* (1998), describe how a real company successfully applied these damage-control strategies. A company that sells healthy, nutritional premium juice emerged from an E. coli outbreak in the mid-1990s comparatively unscathed because of the way it handled the tragic incident, which resulted in the death of a toddler and serious illness in several other people. The company had a reputation for social responsibility and community involvement. Its employees were dedicated to the company, which provided many of the jobs available in the small town in which it is located.

With the crisis threatening its reputation and survival, the company managed to do "the right thing" – both for its customers and for its reputation.

Respond quickly. The company responded quickly to the threat – removing the product suspected of containing the bacterium from store shelves even before the responsibility was confirmed. This was done as soon as the company was informed of a possible link between its product and the outbreak of illnesses caused by the E. coli bacterium.

Organize your response rather than react to individual events. The company quickly organized a crisis management team to make decisions. This was done even before the link between the outbreak and the product was confirmed. The team developed strategies and hired a public relations firm with experience handling such matters.

Inform the public and those with a need to know and keep them informed as new information becomes available. The company called a news conference and issued a press release in a timely manner

– again, even before final confirmation of fault was made. As more information came in, the company continued to keep the public and press informed. The company showed the public what the problem was and how it was being repaired. The company used an Internet site and a 1-800 number to keep in contact with its customers and those who were concerned about the E. coli outbreak.

Take the proper actions called for by the event. The company took concrete steps to manage the problem by locating its source and eliminating it. It also recalled some of its other products treated in the same way just to be sure that the bacterium had not spread and that there would not be any new victims.

Take responsibility for the wrongdoing rather than trying to refocus blame or reduce liability. The company's executives became spokespersons and took responsibility for the problem. They made themselves accessible to the press and issued a formal apology to the public. The company focused on fixing the problem that led to the outbreak and making sure it never happened again rather than on limiting its own liability.

Remember the victim by acting in a responsive, compassionate manner. The company showed concern for those who suffered most from the mistake. Although executives attended the funeral of the child who died, they did not use the event as part of their media campaign to show they cared. They freely offered to pay the medical expenses of the victims and offered refunds to those people who had purchased the company's products and did not feel comfortable in using them.

Re-establish public confidence in your product or

services. Once the immediate crisis was over, the company re-established consumer confidence by reinstating its image and making product changes designed to reassure the public of its commitment to providing healthy beverages.

While the company did eventually face criminal charges and fines in the aftermath of the event, things could have been far worse. It could have lost the public's faith.

What Kind of Things Can Be Done to Enhance an Image?

There are numerous ways to enhance your personal image and that of your organization's. No method is really any better than another, but some are better for certain circumstances than others. Image enhancement is something that must be done carefully, because it can easily backfire on you. Most of us don't consciously go around trying to enhance our standing in the eyes of others. Although we are aware that certain things we do can add or detract from the way others see us, we usually discover this information inadvertently or through a painful experience. By becoming aware of the most common enhancement techniques, and by being aware of their pitfalls as well as their advantages, you will be more likely to meet your objectives.

Image-enhancement techniques include:

- Self-Promotion
- Exemplification
- Association
- Acclaiming
- Attentiveness
- Ingratiation

Because image is so important to your success, so is enhancing that image. A self-promotion strategy, designed to make you look competent, caring, and knowledgeable, is one enhancement technique. Self-promotion must be done in a balanced fashion. You must positively reflect your accomplishments to take credit for them, but you must do so in a way that doesn't provoke negative emotions in others. One way to do this is to have someone else make the promotional claims on your behalf. In fact, these are often seen as more reliable.

An exemplification strategy involves making an example through the behaviors you demonstrate. Individuals can do this by working late, taking on extra work, improving morale, and other activities that promote one's dedication. While this can increase rewards, it also is a danger if these activities are advertised too much. If, for whatever reason, a person fails to live up to the behavior, his credibility can be damaged. Exemplification can help create a corporate culture which promotes attitudes and values that lead to its success.

Association is a strategy where you enhance your image by associating yourself with others who are viewed positively. This rests on the notion that you are often evaluated in light of the company you keep. Acclaiming is an identity-enhancing technique which involves projecting notions about your activities which increase your positive associations with these events. There are two mechanisms for doing this:

•   Entitlements, in which you attempt to link

Image-Enhancement Techniques

- **Self-Promotion**
- **Exemplification**
- **Association**
- **Acclaiming**
- **Attentiveness**
- **Ingratiation**

yourself to a positive occurrence by noting
the role you played in its outcome.

• Enhancements, which you use to maximize
the perceived value of a positive outcome by
emphasizing its strong points.

But, if used indiscreetly, acclaiming strategies can backfire.
For purposes of credibility, it is helpful to have a third-party make the
acclamation – this is what happens when someone introduces a
speaker, for example.

Attentiveness is a highly effective strategy. Focusing attention on an observer makes him feel that his concerns are important,
and that you care about him. This, in turn, heightens the observer's
positive evaluation of you.

Ingratiation is one of the most widespread image-enhancing
techniques, and it may be one of the most effective as well as the
most dangerous. It is accomplished through behaviors designed to
place yourself in a favorable light with others. There are several techniques for doing this:

• Opinion Conformity – This takes place
when we try to make ourselves as similar to
another as possible in attitudes, beliefs, and
values. Sometimes, it is simply a matter of
agreeing with another person. This is a technique often used when trying to establish a
rapport with someone. Using it incorrectly,
however, can have a negative result, making
you appear deceptive or false.

• Favors – The best kind of favors to give others are those which are not easily repaid,
because this can lead to a reciprocal arrange-
ment. Money can easily be repaid, but if you
do something like edit a document for your
employer, you might be repaid by being

viewed more positively and all the benefits that come with it.

- Flattery and Compliments – Complimenting another to show that you value his judgment or characteristics is another effective technique and increases the likelihood that you will be viewed positively by that person. Insincere or overbearing flattery, however, can have an extremely negative effect, and it is usually highly transparent. Sometimes, the only person who is unaware that everybody can see through the flatterer is the flatterer himself. Try following these guidelines when using flattery:

  - Avoid using flattery before a significant event such as a performance evaluation. Even if you are sincere, your motivations may be questioned.

  - Avoid overusing flattery and compliments. This can make them seem insincere.

  - Compliment others on the things which you genuinely view as positive about their performance. The use of genuine compliments will bolster their perceived sincerity and value.

  - Maintain balance and straightforwardness in your approach to compliments. When appropriate, mix compliments with constructive criticism.

- Self-Enhancement – This is a method of por-
traying yourself in ways which you know
that the evaluator finds positive. You would
have to know enough about the other to
make these determinations. This behavior
must be believable, so make sure it is based
on fact or is verifiable.

When applying ingratiation strategies, it is helpful to use the
following guidelines:

- Use ingratiation in situations where it is likely to be acceptable.

- Use ingratiation with other strategies – apply
it in a subtle fashion.

- Emphasize obstacles to your successful performance – show that you were able to overcome obstacles.

- De-emphasize power differences between
you and a superior, and don't use these tactics in situations where the differences are
highlighted.

Chapter Eight Summary

Everybody has to practice "damage control" at times. The
success of your actions will almost invariably depend on the reputation that you previously established. This also applies on the organizational level. If your company has a good reputation, it will be more
likely to survive even the most damaging of events.

In the event of a public relations disaster, you need to help
your organization ensure that its customers come back and are confident in the products and services provided. To do this most effectively, all aspects of the way your organization is run and how employ-

ees act are of critical importance.

Key elements to remember from Chapter Eight include:

√   While a mistake may not seem like a big deal to you, the customer or "victim" of the mistake will probably feel otherwise. If not handled correctly, you could lose that person's respect and business forever.

√   Your reputation is as important to your employer as it is to yourself. The image you project personally can impact your career and future, and it can also affect how the public perceives your organization. This is particularly true in smaller industries and communities.

√   The way in which you apologize or account for your actions is often as important as why the mistake occurred in the first place.

√   A company's reputation is not just affected by how its customer service representatives act. The way it treats its employees and the way in which it makes itself a part of the community impacts the way it is perceived and will play a role in how the public reacts to a serious problem. Therefore, every aspect of an organization's collective behavior should be considered as part of its overall image.

√   During times of crisis in an organization, the behavior of all its employees takes on added importance.

√   Image-enhancement strategies can work on both a personal and organizational level to help you establish a strong reputation to begin with and re-establish it more readily in the event of a crisis.

√   Never, ever take things personally.

√   Remember that you are doing this for your own health, safety, well-being, and future.

CHAPTER NINE

Customer Service
Over the Telephone

"On speech-making. If you don't strike oil
in 20 minutes, stop boring."
– Andrew Carnegie

New Technology Isn't
Always the Best Answer

Telephones, e-mail, and fax-support have become attractive components of providing service in today's technological times. Some providers are simply more comfortable providing information through these mediums. But, when communication is handled through these handy devices, something is lost – the human component.

When people can see one another, they can assess the non-verbal messages the other is sending. While telephone technology is already beginning to address this issue through video phones, change takes a long time and is sometimes never embraced. (Consider that some parts of Colorado had four-party telephone lines until the mid-1990s – and many elderly residents complained when the phone company provided them with private service.) When nonverbal messages cannot be conveyed, the opportunity for misunderstandings increases. A statement is not softened by an unseen smile, and a confused facial expression cannot let a telephone operator know that his instructions have been misunderstood.

The problem becomes even more intense when service is provided via e-mail or fax-support services. On the telephone, a service provider and the member of the public at least have vocal inflections. But these are absent entirely in the written medium, and it is extremely easy to misunderstand another person's meaning. If a person is in a negative mood when he reads such a message, he is likely to read negative connotations into the message, for example. Internet users have attempted to overcome this problem by developing a set of symbols and rules that impart a wink, a smile, a frown, a teardrop, shouting, laughter, and other emotions and nuances. But this language is not known to all, and not everybody is as proficient in the written medium. Service over the Internet and via e-mail are discussed more thoroughly in Chapter Ten.

Services provided in electronic fashion can prove to be greatly frustrating to many people who simply are not good at navigating today's technological tools – they want to talk to a real, breathing person who can empathize with their problems. So, while many helpful services can be provided through fax machines, web pages, and e-mail support systems, the personal touch of human interaction will always be a vital component in satisfying the public.

Telephones

Telephones are the compromise between personal interaction and convenience and will therefore probably always be a major tool for service providers. Because of the problems posed by the lack of nonverbal messages, vocal behaviors and word usage take on added significance during interactions with the public.

The following suggestions are applicable to any telephone interaction in a professional setting, but they are particularly helpful to people who provide services to the general public.

Things To Do

•   **Greet the Caller** – Try to make the person feel that you are happy you can be of assistance, and that you are truly happy to meet him or her. Try to establish a rapport and put the person at case.

•   **Identify Yourself** – When answering the phone, tell the person your name. When calling others, immediately identify yourself, your company, and the purpose for your call.

•   **Speak Clearly** – A bad connection can make it difficult for the customer to interpret the message correctly.

•   **Listen** – Make appropriate responses and let the customer know you understand him, even if you just use an occasional "uh-huh" or "yes" while he is speaking. Avoid interrupting the other speaker.

- **Take Name Hints** – If your callers identify themselves, use the names they give (such as Mrs. Smith or Dr. Thomas). If the person gives you a full name such as Tom Jones, ask for permission to call him "Tom."

- **Seek Clarification if Necessary** – If you feel you have not understood the customer's message, or if you don't think you heard correctly, do not hesitate to ask for further information.

- **Request Feedback** – Because there are no nonverbal communication cues, it may not be apparent that you are expecting a response.

- **Manage Silences** – You must remain silent long enough to allow another to think and to make a response. The practitioner should explain any pauses that occur at other times – such as when looking something up in a computer. A customer, especially one who called in a frustrated state of mind, could possibly interpret a silence in a negative way.

- **Consider Your Location** – Effective communication will be more difficult to achieve if background noise becomes an annoyance or privacy is an issue.

- **Be Sure to Let the Customer Know How to Recontact You** – This is particularly important in a big company with a lot of support personnel. This assures the customer that he or she will not have to start all over again if a return call on the same problem is necessary.

- **Let the Customer Know What You are Doing** – For example, if you are transferring the call, tell the customer the name and number of the person he is being referred to and tell him how this person will be able to help him. In this way, if the connection is inadvertently broken, the customer will know exactly what to do to minimize the reconnection time.

- **Be Prepared For the Difficult Customer** – Know what to do when a challenging caller is on the line. For example, to help yourself adjust to speakers with accents, start with questions that can be answered "yes" or "no" and then graduate to more detailed questions as you become used to the person's manner of speaking.

- **Thank the Customer** – Thank the caller for his patience or for bringing the problem to your attention. Make him feel that he is appreciated. Ask if there is anything else you can do.

- **Let the Caller End the Interaction** – Make sure everything is handled as thoroughly as possible, and let the caller end things. Let him hang up first to be extra sure that you don't inadvertently cut him off.

Things To Avoid

- **Avoid Terms and Statements That May Be Considered Insulting or Condescen-**

ding – This includes terms such as "you girls" or "Hon" or statements like "I thought everybody knew that." While you might consider the use to be innocuous, the customer might take offense.

- **Avoid Taking "Political" Sides** – Unless, of course, it is pertinent to your work. The term in this sense can be applied to everything from a comment about your favorite baseball team to a joke that demonstrates your political affiliation. This can unnecessarily alienate a person with whom you are otherwise relating to well.

- **Don't Make Assumptions** – It is easy to jump to conclusions about others, especially when they initially seem similar to ourselves. But different social and economic backgrounds, along with varied beliefs, impact the communication process. When speaking to a person over the telephone, any of these differences that may be apparent in a face-to-face conversation will not be evident. An extreme example of this might be one related to race, gender, religion, *etc*. If a person made an injudicious comment that could be construed as an insult, it could do the worker and the company untold damages.

- **Don't Make Promises You Can't Keep** – For example, don't agree to do a "special service" for someone unless you are prepared to follow through with that promise.

- **Avoid the Hold Button** – Whenever possible, avoid putting a customer on hold. If it is

The Right Way to Put Someone On Hold

- Always let the customer know what you are doing, particularly if you are going to put him on hold.

- Tell the customer why he is being put on hold and how long it will take.

- Ask the customer if it is okay.

- Give the customer the opportunity to object to being put on hold.

- When you return, thank the customer for waiting.

necessary, ask for permission or offer to call back instead. If it is necessary to put the person on hold, tell him how long it will be and check back with the customer if it looks like it will take longer.

- **If Possible, Avoid Taking Other Callers** – This will emphasize the fact that you think the customer's concerns are important.

- **Don't Turn Your Ears Off** – When encountering a caller with a foreign accent, don't allow yourself to turn off your ability to listen. Treat the interaction as an exercise in listening. If you don't understand something the person says, ask her to repeat it – it is okay to interrupt in this situation. Don't tell

The Right Way to Transfer a Call

- Always let the customer know what you are doing.

- Explain why you are transferring the caller and who you are transferring him to.

- Ask the customer if it is okay.

- Make sure there is a person at the other end of the transfer before you hang up.

- Make sure that other person knows who he will be talking to and what the situation is.

- Accidents happen. Tell the customer how to reconnect with *you* if his needs are not met or if the connection is lost.

the person with the foreign accent to "slow down." Instead, ask the person to rephrase what he is saying or repeat what you did hear and ask for clarification or confirmation.

Cultivating the Voice as a Service Tool

When you provide service over the telephone, a whole dimension of communication disappears, and all that is left are words and the voices which speak them. This can have a dramatic impact on what the customer perceives. Vocal attributes are particularly crucial over the phone when we do not personally know the other person, and these attributes are the only means the service provider and consumer have to interpret meanings.

In a face-to-face meeting with another person, body language makes up 55 percent of the total message, while vocal tones give 38 percent and words add the final 7 percent. But, over the telephone, both take on added importance, and vocal tones make up 86 percent of the overall message. From this, it should be clear that you have to be very careful how you present what you have to say.

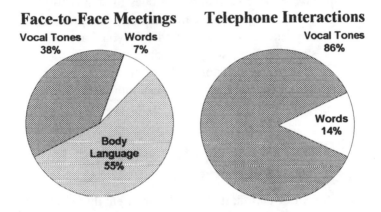

Because phones can distort voices, a person can be entirely unaware of the impact his tone is having on the impression the other person is forming. If your job requires you to communicate with the public regularly via the telephone, you might want to record yourself to find out how you sound to others. In any event, it should be clear that how you use your voice is very important to the outcome of the process.

In general, your voice should be:

- **Pleasant** – Particularly when the other person is not. Remaining calm will enable you to manage the behavior of the other so that he will likely begin to communicate in a similar, calm, pleasant way necessary for a productive conversation. Also, listening to a "recitation" is not pleasant, so cultivate a conversational tone of voice.

- **Interested** – You should sound as if you care and are ready, willing, and able to assist the other person. Your voice should communicate your interest through its expressiveness. Vary your rate and tones.

- **Understandable** – Because there are no nonverbal communication cues to help convey messages, take care to clearly and properly enunciate your words. If you have a strong accent, work to make it conform to your average customer. If the customer has a strong accent, however, don't mimic it.

What Your Tone of Voice Tells Others

From this information, it should be apparent that how a word is said is as important as which word is used. The voice can signal extroversion or introversion, dominance or submission, and likes or dislikes. It can reveal turn-taking preferences in a conversation and provide information on gender, age, and race. Furthermore, the voice can inform others about attitudes, and specific sounds which express accent and dialect can influence judgments and help distinguish social class, prestige, and power. The most apparent attributes of sound that convey messages and provide measurable functions in interpersonal communication are:

1. **Loudness** – The amplitude of sound is measured in decibels to indicate the acoustic energy reaching a receiver.

2. **Pitch** – Emotion influences pitch. For example,

The Right Way to Take Messages

- Always explain that the person wanted is unavailable – then take the caller's name.

- Give positive, general reasons for the absence of the desired person. For example, say "He stepped out of the office" or "He is on vacation" rather than "I don't know where he is" or "He's sick."

- Make sure the message is complete and legible. Get area codes and proper names and titles.

- Give the caller an estimate of when the person will be back.

- Offer to help the caller yourself or transfer him to someone who can help.

- Don't sound as if you are rushed. Treat the caller as if his call is of the utmost importance.

a person who is sad or stunned is most likely to speak with a lower pitch, while excitement and gaiety are expressed by a higher pitch. Anger can be expressed in a quiet, low pitch or in a louder, high pitch.

3.   **Rate** – The number of sounds emitted during a given unit of time or the speed with which one speaks is referred to as rate. Rate of speech can convey how fluent a speaker is as well as the intensity of the message.

4.   **Quality** – Vocal quality allows us to distinguish one person's voice from another and can strongly impact the impression made by that person. To another person a breathy voice may indicate shallowness and superficial meanings, while a flat voice may indicate sluggishness, coolness, or withdrawal.

5.   **Articulation** – Careful articulation, necessary for effective communication, is defined by specific vowel or consonant sounds and by the syllables that are emphasized.

6.   **Pronunciation** – Specific vowel or consonant sounds and emphasis of syllables in words are related to pronunciation. Correct and consistent pronunciation is necessary for effective communication.

7.   **Silence** – While silence is not an attribute of vocal cues, it serves a vital function in interpersonal communication, as it is considered an effective response in communicative interactions. Silence can express anxiety and can be used to convey such messages as defiance or annoyance.

Things to Do, Things to Avoid
When it Comes to Your Voice

Like any other type of behavior, your voice is a tool you can

Handling Vulgarity Over the Telephone

1. Ignore the first outburst and try to change things by setting an example with your own calm, professional behavior.

    Example: "Thank you for bringing this problem to my attention, sir. I'll help you in any way I can."

2. Continue to try to help, but politely tell the customer that you are having difficulty with the language being used.

    Example: "Sir, I can help you with that, but I'm not used to that kind of language."

3. If the use of vulgar language persists, restate your objections. Remember to use words that don't place blame. ("I am having trouble with. . . ." rather than "You are using bad language.")

    Example: "I apologize again. I just don't work well when this kind of language is being used."

4. Give up. You have done your best. Explain to the caller that you are no longer able to help him and will transfer him to a supervisor. Always follow transfer etiquette to leave a final good impression of your professionalism.

train with practice. Here are some of the things to keep in mind:

Things To Do

- Smile when you are speaking on the phone. This improves your vocal tones.

- Practice varying your vocal tones so that you don't sound like you are in a rut. Learn to stress certain words and exaggerate your tones.

- Think about the statements you make regularly when interacting with the public, and consider how you can say them in a way that positively impacts the interaction. For example, read the following sentences out loud, changing the vocal emphasis you place on the words according to which ones are italicized:

  - What can I do to help you? (no inflection/monotone)
  - *What* can I do to help you?
  - What *can* I do to help you?
  - What can *I* do to help you?
  - What can I *do* to help you?
  - What can I do to *help* you?
  - What can *I* do to help *you*?

  Each of these vocal inflections dramatically changes the meaning of the sentence.

- Breathe. When people are under stress, their breathing becomes more shallow. Taking deep breaths will help you improve your vocal tones.

- Match the customer's rate of speaking and intensity of feeling to try to help him feel at ease. If a person speaks in a slower manner than you are used to, it's *your* job to slow down.

- Use relaxed, natural tones when speaking to others.

- People who use a relatively fast speaking rate with an appropriate volume are generally considered more credible than those who seem deliberately slow.

- Use short pauses during the course of your conversation.

- If you have an accent that differs significantly from the typical person you serve, realize that a barrier is present and attempt to conform to the standard accent or learn to compensate so that the barrier is minimized. Learn to recognize situations in which your accent is a problem for your client.

- Your voice should be warm and relaxed, yet expressive, dynamic, and animated. Your voice should be confident, friendly, and pleasant. Be sure to use your voice in a way that expresses your sincere interest in the other person.

- Have something to drink on hand whenever you need to speak on the telephone. When you are under stress, your voice may become hoarse. Drink something to alleviate this so that you can maintain your most pleasant vocal tones.

- Your laughter should be genuine and appropriate. Avoid false, insincere laughter.

Things To Avoid

- Avoid using a monotone voice. It implies that you are bored.

- Don't sound as if you are an actor or actress reciting a script. Use a natural conversational tone.

- Don't speak too slowly. It implies that you would rather be left alone.

- Don't be too abrupt. Abrupt speaking in loud tones tells others that you are angry.

- Avoid terms such as "um," "er," "sort of," "oh, well," and "like."

- Don't use vocal tones that are inconsistent with your verbal message.

- Interrupting the other person implies that you are not interested in what he has to say. Even if your purpose is to keep the conversation on track, avoid interruptions.

- Don't allow vocal tones which suggest anger, irritation, boredom, or other negative emotions to enter your interactions.

- A tense voice can cause a negative reaction in others.

- Avoid overlapping speech when the client is speaking.

- Don't address the other in an overly formal manner.

- Avoid speaking in a non-general, regionally specific dialect because it can pose a barrier for communication. If you do speak with an accent, be careful to ensure that the other can understand you.

- Avoid using slang that others may not understand. Don't use meaningless particles such as "you know."

- Hesitating, hedging, or not being fluent in your speech can make you seem less credible.

- Avoid the lack of positive vocal reinforcement or the absence of vocal warmth. Don't use a narrow range of pitch or volume.

- Failing to laugh when appropriate is extremely negative, but so is laughter at inappropriate times. False or phony laughter is to be avoided.

Chapter Nine Summary

In today's technological era, electronic methods of providing service have become more and more common. Face-to-face interaction is becoming correspondingly less common. The telephone has become an intermediate form of service, and it will probably remain the service method of choice in the future. For this reason, its peculiarities cannot be ignored by those who serve the public.

Key elements to remember from Chapter Nine include:

√ When using electronic devices to provide support, a necessary "human component" is lost.

√   Since nonverbal messages cannot be read by the customer and the service provider, vocal information takes on added importance in the telephone interaction.

√   Never, ever take things personally.

√   Remember that you are doing this for your own health, well-being, safety, and future.

CHAPTER TEN

Customer Service on the Internet

*"Kind words can be short and easy to speak,
but their echoes are truly endless."*

Mother Teresa

The Internet – Not Just a Fad in Providing Customer Service
What is So Powerful About Providing Service Over the Internet?
Internet 101: Everything You Wanted to Know Without the Techno-
    Speak
What is an Internet or Web Page?
What Information Should be Included in an Internet Site?
Just the FAQs – the All-Important FAQs
E-mail – A Dangerous Tool in the Wrong Hands
Isn't This Just Giving People Another Way to Complain?

The Internet – Not Just a Fad in Providing Customer Service

To those uninitiated in the latest technologies, Internet pages may seem like an expensive fad. But to those who are comfortable with the changes wrought by the Information Age, the Internet is a vital communication tool that should not be overlooked. This chapter discusses both the development of Internet sites for customer service purposes and the development of the unique skills needed for interacting with customers via this medium.

What is So Powerful About Providing Service Over the Internet?

Companies and organizations across the world are learning the value of using the Internet to communicate with their clients. At first, this communication medium was used by most as a way to advertise their products and services. But the strength of this medium really lies in its use as a way of providing two-way communication. You can communicate directly with your customers, and they can communicate with you.

Many companies and organizations make the mistake of designing their pages without interactivity in mind. This defeats the purpose of the Internet. You might as well just publish that type of information in a manual. By using this medium, you can perform many service functions, including:

- Answering Customer Questions

- Solving Your Customers' Problems

- Showing Your Customers that You Care About Their Concerns

- Selling Your Products

- Educating Your Customers About the Use of

Your Products and Services

- Getting Feedback

- Offering a Forum for Complaints

- Getting Ideas for Developing Future Products

Now, you can even have face-to-face meetings with your clients via the Internet. This type of technology can be used to educate your customers or help them with their problems in their own homes by showing them how to do something and walking them through it. Not every company will find this type of service necessary, or even desirable, but it does illustrate the kind of quick, timely assistance you can offer.

People have become accustomed to instant service. They don't want to have to wait to get their problems solved. By using the Internet, you give them the ability to do this. If your site is adequate, most will be less frustrated even if they can't find the answer to their particular question, because at least they know you tried, and at least they will now know what to do to get the help they need.

Internet 101: Everything You Wanted to Know Without the Techno-Speak

The Internet is a world-wide system of computers linked together in a vast network through modems, cables, telephone lines, and satellites. It began as a system to allow scientists to share their findings. When you access your server through your computer, you are connecting to an unregulated system of information that criss-crosses the globe and allows you virtually instant access to any other computer in the world. Rather than having to go to the library to access an out-of-date encyclopedia, you have instant and immediate access to the latest information about your subject. You can make your travel arrangements, buy theater tickets, do your banking, buy a car, and entertain yourself without leaving your desk.

190 Chapter Ten – Service on the Internet

What *is* an Internet Site or Web Page?

Internet sites – also known as web pages – are an incredibly valuable and cost-efficient tool to service providers and organizations of all types. With these pages, your customers can have immediate access to service. They no longer have to place expensive phone calls or wait in long lines. They don't have to wait for the weekend to end or for your office hours to begin. When they want service, they can get it immediately.

Web pages are not the answer to all your customer service problems, but they are designed to help the do-it-yourselfer, enabling you to spend more time and resources assisting those customers seeking more traditional client support. But, like any tool, the Internet can be misused. If you do not understand it and use its capabilities in the most appropriate and effective ways, your efforts can backfire.

What Information Should be Included in an Internet Site?

While you must provide honest, accurate information on your web pages and in your e-mail responses, you must be discreet. Embarrassing information can be used against you or your organization by your competitors and the press. For this reason, you must treat these forums as public documents. When you strike a balance between complete openness and discretion, you will generate respect for your site and service.

More information on managing troublesome situations your organization may be facing is presented elsewhere in this book. Your web site can be valuable in helping you overcome serious public relation problems.

The information you include in your web site depends on your organization and what the public will expect or want. Your customers may be at the office, they may work at home – either way, if they are seeking customer service, they are using valuable time they'd rather spend doing something else. Make sure the information you provide is worth that time.

If your customers cannot find the information they want quickly and conveniently, they may not come back to your site the next time they need information.

- Don't put so much on your web page that a user has difficulty finding the help section or figuring out how to use it.

- Have an e-mail address the user can write to if he cannot find the solution to his problem on the page.

- Remember that technology changes faster than many people can afford to keep up with. If a customer e-mails you to say he is having difficulty accessing your support pages, don't tell him it's too bad he has outdated equipment – try to help him resolve his problem.

- Don't just suggest that the customer take a closer look at the help pages and ignore his question. Even if the answer to his problem is clearly detailed on your support pages, answer as if his problem is unique and that you are happy to help him. Send him the solution rather than making him search the

What is a Search Engine?

A search engine is a tool that allows your customers to enter a key word or a few key words that are used to quickly connect them to files and information that include those words.

pages. He may be contacting your e-mail address because he is uncomfortable with support pages or is not experienced at Internet navigation.

• Provide a search engine that the customer can use to quickly find information (if your site is really small, a table of contents may be enough).

• Let the customer know right up front what is available at your site.

• Don't design the site based on what you want to tell your customer; base it on what the customer wants to know.

Just the FAQs – the All-Important FAQs

One way in which customers can be serviced via the Internet is through FAQs. Your FAQs are files that contain the answers to those questions most frequently asked by your customers. If you are not a front-line service provider, be sure to include these people in the development of your FAQs. They know what the customer is really asking when he or she requests information.

Your FAQs should change and grow over time as you receive feedback. If you find that you are continuing to get questions about

What is a FAQ?

A FAQ is a file you place on your Internet pages that contains the answers to "Frequently-Asked Questions."

something in your FAQs, then you may not be answering the under-lying question, or the response may be inadequate in some way.

Here are some guidelines you can use when developing your FAQ files:

- FAQs should be well-written and under-standable by any of your customers, from the newest to the most sophisticated.

- These files should be well-organized. You might want to have several FAQ files based on your customers' needs. For example, you might have basic answers and answers for advanced users of your products. To make your customers feel special, you might want a FAQ section for your registered customers only. A more basic format can be used by your potential customers.

- If you do have a separate section for regis-tered users, make sure there is a way for your customers to get in if they forget their passwords.

- If you offer many products or services, con-sider having separate FAQ files and cus-tomer service e-mail addresses for each.

- Remember that it is the answers that are important. If you "dress up" your FAQ pages, be sure that it doesn't detract from quick access to the information. These peo-ple may be frustrated – don't make them push four or five buttons to get to informa-tion you promised them at the first button.

- FAQs should be easy to locate and access from your web page.

- FAQs should be kept up to date.

- FAQs should include enough information to help the majority of the people who ask the question.

- FAQ files should not be dated. Even if the information is up-to-date, the reader might not think so if an old date is on the file.

- Cater your FAQ files to your known customers rather than to the casual Internet surfer.

- Don't promise that your FAQs will provide what they do not.

E-mail – A Dangerous Tool in the Wrong Hands

E-mail has become one of the major tools of the workplace, rivaling even the ever-present memo as a corporate communication device. With the onset of free e-mail services that can be used from any public-access computers connected to the Internet, anybody who wants an e-mail address can have one.

E-mail is a valuable customer service tool because it provides a way to quickly send messages and get responses. Rather than waiting more than a week for a response, and rather than waiting to get the time to go somewhere to get service, your customers can get a response the same day.

If a customer does not receive a response to her concerns in a timely manner, she will think one of three things:

- That the e-mail or response to it got lost.

- That the company doesn't care about her concerns.

What is E-Mail?

E-mail – which is short for "Electronic Mail" – is the ultra-fast equivalent of the letters you send through the Post Office (regular mail is known as "snail mail" to those who have become used to the speed of e-mail). When you have an e-mail account, you can send and receive private letters and messages in a matter of moments, rather than writing out a letter, putting it in an envelope, stamping it, taking it to the Post Office, and waiting several days for it to reach its destination.

- Or that the company is too busy to respond.

No matter which way the customer thinks, your disorganization will discourage her from remaining a customer if an acceptable alternative is presented to her.

Consider programming your system to automatically respond to e-mail messages with a form letter that thanks the customer for his message. It lets the customer know immediately that his message was received and has been forwarded to the proper person. Be sure to identify the message as an automatic response.

You might even include a link in your auto response that connects the customer to your FAQ files. If you do this, assure the customer that his mail will be read by a customer service representative, so his question will be answered if it is not included in the FAQ.

But e-mail can also be dangerous if misused. If you or your employees incorrectly misrepresent your company or position, e-mail can be used against you in court. It is evidence in the same way a letter can be evidence. E-mail will likely involve many issues within your company. The person in charge of answering general e-mail directed at your company may not know the answer or be best qualified to answer all the questions. E-mail should be forwarded to people responsible for particular types of questions. There are software packages that can assist with the categorization and forwarding of e-mail.

Here are some tips about providing access to and answering e-mail directed to your company or organization:

• Treat your customers with respect, even if the e-mail is negative or filled with objectionable language.

• Don't use a service in which the public has no method of responding to the e-mail. If you use an automated system, make sure it is set up so that responses go to a person who can evaluate them.

• Don't send a formal note informing the user that he has e-mailed the wrong address. If he has mailed a note about his problem to the wrong address, send a friendly note that apologizes for the problem and includes the proper address. In addition, forward the letter to the proper address, and let the customer know that you have done this.

• Respond personally whenever possible. As in any customer service interaction, the personal touch is a desirable commodity. People want to talk to the expert. They want to be treated as valuable.

• Don't ignore any e-mail, even if you don't have an answer for the problem. Your failure to respond will be more damaging than saying "I don't know."

• Don't assume that the customer understands Internet language.

- Reread your response and make sure that it will not be misread by a person who is in a negative mood. Be careful how you use humor.

- Don't be overly informal in your e-mail communications. Give every response the proper consideration. Remember that an e-mail response could end up as evidence in court.

- Use paragraphs, indents, and line spaces to make your message more readable.

- Use a separate paragraph for each thought, and keep your paragraphs short.

- Choose your words carefully.

- Use descriptive subject lines to make it stand out to your customers.

- Don't make promises that you and your organization cannot keep.

- Try to stick to one subject in your e-mail messages.

- Mirror back your customers' concerns in your responses, or include a copy of the original message at the end of the response to remind the customer of his question.

- Establish a company policy concerning e-mail that sets guidelines regarding professionalism and rules.

- It is recommended that employees not use

company e-mail for personal reasons. Otherwise, a company policy should be in place, and it might be a good idea to attach a disclaimer signature line to personal e-mail.

• Be aware of legal issues regarding your company's particular products and services. Be careful that your responses don't commit your organization to a legal responsibility. Refer the e-mail to a higher authority within your organization if there is any possibility of a legal question arising.

• Don't make people search for your e-mail address. It should be accessible from every place on your web page.

• Respond to customer e-mail within 24 hours – this meets customer expectations.

• Never send e-mail to your customers without their permission. Some people have to pay for each e-mail they receive.

Isn't This Just Giving People Another Way to Complain?

Complaints are valuable things. People who take the time to complain are showing you that they care. They want you to be able to fix the problem. This is a customer you can keep. The unhappy customer who does not bother to complain to you will probably be going to your competitor the next time he needs to buy the product or service. She may decide to vote against funding for your projects if you are with a governmental organization.

Perhaps the most valuable thing you will receive as a result of providing customer service over the Internet is feedback. People will tell you exactly what they think of your company and its products or services. In face-to-face meetings, and even on the telephone, people are reluctant to be entirely truthful – they may not want to hurt your feelings, or they may not want to take out their frustrations on the customer service clerk. But there are no holds barred in e-mail. The quasi-anonymity of the medium allows people to let down their hair and get all their frustrations off their chest.

You can use this truthful information. You can use it to make a better product than your competitor. You can use it to provide quicker, more efficient service. You can use it to anticipate problems and needs. You can use it to design accessories to sell along with your products or to enhance them. You can use it to identify trends. You can use it to assess your customers for marketing purposes. In fact, there is no end to the number of ways you can use this priceless feedback.

Chapter Ten Summary

Organizations without a presence on the Internet not only miss out on sales opportunities, but they also miss out on a relatively inexpensive way to provide service and keep their customers happy. Organizations whose business mainly consists of information dissemination are particularly missing out if they fail to use this medium to its fullest.

But being dedicated to having an Internet site is not enough. Like any other facet of a business, it must be organized and regulated so that it can operate at its highest level of efficiency.

Key elements to remember from Chapter Ten include:

√   Web page designers and customer service representatives both need to understand the rules of providing service via the Internet and e-mail.

√   The strength of providing service over the Internet is that it can be a two-way communication device.

√   The feedback you receive can give you

information that helps virtually every facet of your organization.

√   Your customers demand instant access to service. You can meet this critical imperative with an adequately designed web page.

√   E-mail is convenient, but often incorrectly used. Establishing strict guidelines and policies for using e-mail can help you protect your company.

√   Never, ever take things personally.

√   Remember that you are doing this for your own health, safety, well-being, and future.

Index